POTENTIAL

POTENTIAL

The Name Analysis Book _____

Paul & Valeta Rice

Samuel Weiser, Inc.
York Beach, Maine

Privately published in 1980
by the F.A.C.E. Association
© 1980 Paul and Valeta Rice

This completely revised edition
first published in 1987 by
Samuel Weiser, Inc.
Box 612
York Beach, Maine 03910

ISBN 0-87728-632-9
Library of Congress Cataloging in Publication Data

Rice, Paul, 1909–
    Potential : the name analysis book.

    Bibliography: p.
    1. Fortune-telling by names. 2. Symbolism of
numbers. I. Rice, Valeta. II. Title.
BF1891.N3R53 1987   133.3'354   86-34015
ISBN 0-87728-632-9

Typeset in 11 point Times Roman
Printed in the United States of America

Contents

About the Authors

If Valeta and Paul Rice sound familiar, it may be because they travel to many cities, ranging from Fairbanks, Alaska, to San Diego, California, and across the continental United States to New York and Maine. During their invitational stopovers, they conduct workshops and seminars about Name Analysis and Birthdate Analysis. They have been conducting these workshops for over twenty years.

The Rices have been interested in occult studies for more than forty years. Starting with a book about ESP their search for esoteric knowledge expanded to include astrology, reincarnation, palmistry, personology, tarot, color, dream analysis, the qabala, meditation, visualization, and healing. While their professions are different— Valeta is a graduate of the University for Humanistic Studies with a major in psychology, while Paul is a graduate of Iowa State University, with a degree in Engineering—they enjoy the cooperation that team teaching provides. Valeta has compiled esoteric knowledge gleaned from the studies previously mentioned, from many seminars as well as from guidance received through meditation. Paul has taught a simplified method of understanding the science of numerology to hundreds who have attended his Name Analysis and Birthdate Analysis classes. They have written fourteen books about numerology and their books have been sold in New Zealand, England, France, Spain, Canada, Poland, Africa, and the U.S.

The Rices conduct seminars on numerology throughout the country. For further information regarding personal readings or seminars, please contact:

Paul and Valeta Rice
F.A.C.E. Association
177 Webster St.
#A105
Monterey, CA 93940

Why Analyze Your Name?

What would it be like if you had a different name? Would the same things happen to you? Would you really be different? Would your talents be different? Would the comings and goings of your life have different paths with different names? Perhaps you would become attached to someone different. Perhaps you could accumulate a fortune with another name. How can we determine these possibilities?

Authorities in various fields have said that we are all surrounded by vibrations. It is possible to tune into vibrations that affect our way of life or our life style. Many wise people also advocate that nothing happens by chance. Everyone has some definite purpose to accomplish in this lifetime. There is a way to become aware and interpret these vibrations through the universal language of numbers.

Numbers are the same, have the same meaning throughout the entire planet. Go to any country and hold up two or three fingers and the native of that country will understand the number even if your language cannot be understood. We live in a mathematical world. Everything is named and numbered and we cannot communicate without numbers. We have social security numbers, house numbers, area code numbers, zip code numbers, phone numbers, birth numbers, car license numbers, and the list goes on and on. Consequently, your knowledge of numbers—their vibrations and interpretations—is quite important.

Pythagoras, a sixth century B.C. mystic, worked with the ratios of musical intervals and led other learned people to suppose that because the musical scale could be expressed in mathematical terms, it was also possible to reduce the essence of all things to a certain vibrational number. While we are not working within the Pythagorean scale, learning the meaning of the numbers will enable you to interpret a "secret code," thus providing you with a knowledge not possessed by others.

Why should one study numbers during these busy times? Most people like to know about themselves, why certain events happen for them, or why they react the way they do. Nothing happens by chance. Even your name was determined before your birth, and your name reflects your personality. Change your name and you change your personality.

I am reminded of a young man and his wife, whom we met late one night in Pasadena, CA, after finishing a workshop at the I.C.C. International Convention. The couple noticed Paul kidding with the waitresses about their birthdates. The wife leaned over and asked, "Do you think you could help us with a problem?" "Sure," and we moved over to their booth. Valeta did a few simple things for them and they invited us to their home. There we saw the fine oil paintings the husband painted.

Valeta compiled the couple's numerological charts and changed the artist's name to correspond with his talents. We had dinner with this couple a year later and the artist told us he had become so successful selling his paintings that it was almost like a miracle, and he attributed his success to the name change. Not only was his name changed, but his attitude toward his business had changed. A definite change in personality, one that enhanced his ability, had occurred.

What else does your name tell you? First, from your name you find out what you would like to do, what your soul urge is, your heart's desire. Once you become aware of these desires it behooves you to pay attention, otherwise indulging in an occupation that is not compatible with your motivations could lead to a frustrating life.

Second, you can see yourself when you are alone and not reacting to stimuli. Your name can help you become aware and admit to what you really are (at this time) so you can see how to best fit your desires to your inner self, or vice versa. You pay attention to your dreams, both night and daytime dreams. This is an important aspect of your character, for today's dreams have been known to become tomorrow's reality for those who dare and are aware.

Third, when you combine your desires with inner self-realization, you can select goals, work, or profession more intelligently, making full use of your potential.

What are your chances of success? When you follow the numerical vibrations of your name, it can lead you into the path that you were born to follow. Your names reveals hidden experiences that have a vital effect on your life. Experiences you have occluded from your conscious memory can reveal your hidden talents and the barriers to accomplishing your goals. All of this information is contained in the vibrations of the letters and numbers of your name.

Not only is this information available for yourself, you can also, through the numerical vibrations of other names, discover better ways of communicating with loved ones, co-workers and spiritual partners. Open the door to your potential!

Discovering the Numbers

One day as I was coming out of a meditative state I became aware of the correlation between numbers, planets, and categories. Astrologers have defined the energies and placement of the planets for centuries. The new information I was given combined the planetary energies with the vibrations of the numbers and their placement in a Numerological Chart or Numeroscope. The following information helps us analyze the name:

1) The number derived from the addition of the vowels in a name also exhibits the energy of the planet Mars.

2) The number derived from the addition of the consonants in a name also exhibits the energy of the Moon.

3) The number derived from the addition of the vowels and consonants in a name is equal to the energy of the astrological ascendant, although this is not a planetary energy.

These concepts will be discussed in detail as we proceed to analyze names.

Categories Used in Name Analysis

In order to understand how we will discuss name analysis, we need to understand the categories involved. The name analysis is based on a study of the vowels, consonants, and the combination of the vowels and consonants. The following list explains how we can add Mars, the Moon, and the Ascendant to these categories.

Vowels (desire): This number is computed from the vowels in your name and represents your motivation in life, your heart's desire, that which your ideal self most wants to do. It symbolizes the motive which lies behind your actions, judgments and attitudes. It represents your individual point of view.

Mars: This planet is connected to your **desire** number, the energy that sets fire to your motivations, the enterprising and sometimes forceful teacher that puts action into your wishes. Mars energy glows with a steady warm flame or it flashes like a laser; the energy expended depends on the number. The negative side of the Mars energy can be expressed as defiance or outright rebellion. Sometimes this energy expresses as sarcasm, overt hostility, or cruelty.

Astrologers know that Mars can appear in any of the twelve signs of the zodiac in your natal chart. When we speak of Mars in relation to a number in your name, we must keep in mind that the number will intensify the natural Mars energy in a chart. For example, if you have Mars in Aries, you will take very different action than someone with Mars in Cancer. If you add the number **4** to Mars in Aries, or Mars in Cancer, you will find that the Aries energy is "steadied" by this number, and the Cancer energy is steadied as well. Therefore, Mars in Aries influenced by a **4** will be a more dependable Mars in Aries—not in such a hurry as people who have Mars in Aries influenced by another number. Likewise, a **6** influence will add the qualities of the **6** to the typical energy indicated by the planet in a certain sign.

Consonants (dormant self): This number is computed from your name and represents your personality—the true you that cannot hide behind a mask. This is you at rest when you are by yourself and away from all outside influences. This also symbolizes the dreamer—indicating your fantasies about yourself if you are not honest in the evaluation of yourself.

Moon: This luminary is connected to your **dormant self** number, the energy that is sensitive, clever, imaginative and perceptive. This considerate side of your personality can be tolerant and kind. Negative Moon energy can bring emotional outbursts. Used negatively, this is the part of yourself that worries and becomes moody at times.

Astrologers know that the Moon can appear in any of the twelve signs. When a number is influenced by the Moon, two things are happening: the number influences the sign the Moon is in for better or worse. Sometimes the quality of the number will help the Moon sign, and sometimes you may need to be aware that the number aggravates characteristics that are symbolized by a certain Moon sign. When you analyze a person, keep in mind that you may need to explain how this energy may affect the Moon responses.

Vowels and Consonants Combined (abilities): This number is computed from your entire name and represents your natural potentials, the type of work or profession in which you could excel, a promise of opportunities in your chosen field of endeavor.

Astrological Ascendant: This is the energy that is connected to your **abilities** number. The rising sign in the horoscope tells us how we differ in temperament and physical appearance from other people. The individuality of our experiences and the way we respond to them colors our viewpoint. It also solidifies our attitudes towards others. On the negative side, this number can represent judgment of others as we evaluate people through our experience.

In order to learn what your ascendant is, you need to have your astrological chart computed correctly. You need to know your day, month, and year of birth, as well as the location of your birth (city and state), plus the time of day you were born.* When your chart is cast,

---

*There are a number of computer services available to anyone who wants to have the chart calculated mathematically. These services do not provide any interpretation; they only cast the horoscope for you so you can learn the signs and planets involved in your chart. A listing of these services will be found in the Appendix.

Table 1. Number Categories

Category	Derived from	Planetary Energy
Desire	Vowels	Mars
Dormant Self	Consonants	Moon
Abilities	Vowels and Consonants Combined	Ascendant

you will discover that one of the twelve zodiacal signs is on the cusp of your first house, which is the ascendant. When you understand the basic characteristics of the twelve signs, you will see how the numbers relate to this sign. The number may make you stronger than the average person with Pisces rising, for example, or your number may indicate that you are more frivolous than one usually might be with this ascendant.

• • •

To review what we have just discussed, see Table 1 for a brief listing of the categories. You will have to learn these by heart if you want to thoroughly get involved in casting Numeroscopes.

The Combinations

Combinations of numbers (in the whole name) taken before they are reduced to a single digit have a certain significance. This significance lets us interpret how one's vibrations progress toward the expression of a single digit. Each person's name has an individuality, as shown in the examples that follow.

Example 1: Jane

1	5		9					Vowels = 15/6
J	a	n	e	S	m	i	t	h	=
1	5			1	4		2	8	Consonants = 21/3

Total = 36/9

Example 2: Mia

9	1		1	5	Vowels = 16/7
M	i	a	D	a	c	e =
4			4	3	Consonants = 11/2

Total = 27/9

Jane and Mia approach their total expression or **Abilities** from two different directions. Jane approaches her humanitarianism (**9**) from the base of an outgoing attitude (**3**), coupled with a need for harmony (**6**). Mia approaches her humanitarianism (**9**) from a base of cooperation (**2**), coupled with an analytical attitude (**7**).

We call this approach to the final single digit number *the combinations*. This approach can be used for name analysis and birthdate analysis.

The Numbers

The following pages contain short interpretations of the basic vibrations of each number from **1** through **66**. Once you have looked at the basic definitions of the numbers you can begin to compute the value of your birth name. The first three categories we will discuss are desire numbers, dormant-self numbers, and ability numbers. Each of these categories will have a separate interpretation for numbers **1** through **66**. We also include a discussion of the various number combinations, so you will have an even better understanding of the more complex numbers and how they affect your life.

As you study the numbers, their categories, and their planet vibrations, we suggest that you start learning the single digit interpretations before you move to the compound numbers. Some of you may not be familiar with how to determine your numbers from the letters in your name. Each letter has a numerical value that is based on the alphabet. Table 2 on page 12 shows you how to easily determine your vowels and consonants according to traditional numerology.

There are three levels to the interpretation of every number: positive, negative, repressive. This does not mean that everyone expresses on all three levels. You can evaluate how you express

Table 2. Numerological Values of Vowels and Consonants

1	2	3	4	5	6	7	8	9
A	B	C	D	E	F	G	H	I
J	K	L	M	N	O	P	Q	R
S	T	U	V	W	X	Y	Z	

yourself by observing how you react in certain situations. What is your chronic emotional tone? Are you happy, grumpy, short-tempered, enthusiastic, fearful, bored? Look at the suggested interpretations shown in Table 3 and see where you fit in. People with the same numbers react differently to situations and differ in attitude towards themselves and others because numbers can express on different levels. You can see the level you operate on and change that level if you wish to change yourself. You can also change your name, or a few letters in your name, to bring in the vibrations of your choice. Students should memorize the positive, negative and repressive meanings of each of the basic numbers. Note we have also included the Master numbers, and as these are more unusual, we have added keywords to help you understand their special significance.

Table 3. Positive, Negative, and Repressive Energy

Positive	Negative	Repressive
Certain	Apathetic	Despotic
Enthusiastic	Unsure	Suppressive
Definite	Antagonistic	Tyrannical
Specific	Vacillating	Hostile
Searching	Non-feeling	Violent
Transforming	Covert	Stifling
Activating	Resentful	Hateful

Number 1

Positive: Creative, optimistic, self-determined, creative mind through feeling, can reach a higher dimension of awareness when preceded by a **10**, rebirth.

Negative: Indecisive, arrogant, a fabricator.

Repressive: Tyrannical, hostile, ill-willed.

Number 2

Positive: Sensitive, rhythmic, patient, restful, skilled, responsive to emotional appeal with love; protective, a lover, a peacemaker.

Negative: Unfeeling, impatient, cowardly, overly sensitive about self.

Repressive: Mischievous, self-deluded, hostile, paranoid.

Number 3

Positive: Communicative, entertaining, can acquire knowledge from higher beings, charming, inspirational, an intuitive counselor.

Negative: Conceited, prone to exaggeration, dabbles but never really learns anything exactly, gossips, a dilettante.

Repressive: Hypocritical, intolerant, wasteful, jealous, prejudicial.

Number 4

Positive: Good organizer, devoted to duty, loyal, orderly, has great endurance, able to heal etheric body by magnetism which works on higher levels.

Negative: Inflexible, a plodder, penurious, stiff, clumsy, rigid, argumentative.

Repressive: Hateful, suppressive, needs to get even, vulgar.

Number 5

Positive: Adventurous, understanding, clever, has the essence of life, creative mentality, a traveler, capable of creative healing.

Negative: Inconsistent, self-indulgent, tasteless, inelegant, sloppy.

Repressive: Perverted, indulges in alcohol or drugs, afraid of change, lacks sympathy for others.

Number 6

Positive: Harmonious, has good judgment, loves home and family, balanced, a cosmic mother, self-realized, represents a doorway to higher mind through harmony, has a metaphysical mind.

Negative: Anxious, interfering, careless.

Repressive: Cynical, nasty, involved in domestic tyranny.

Number 7

Positive: Analytical, refined, studious, has inner wisdom; the number symbolizes a bridge from the mundane to the esoteric, a mystic, can heal spiritual gaps.

Negative: Confused, skeptical, aloof, a contender or one who humiliates others.

Repressive: Malicious, a cheater, ignorant, suppressive of self and others.

Number 8

Positive: Powerful, a leader, dependable, a chief or director, handles money well, full of primal energy, can open third eye, see auras.

Negative: Intolerant, biased, scheming, loves power-fame-glory, impatient.

Repressive: A bigot, abusive, an oppressor, weak.

Number 9

Positive: Compassionate, charitable, aware, romantic, successful, humane, a humanitarian, merciful, involved with the brotherhood of man.

Negative: Selfish, unkind, scornful, stingy, unforgiving, indiscreet, inconsiderate.

Repressive: Bitter, morose, dissipated, immoral.

Number 11

Positive: Idealistic, intuitive, cerebral, spiritual, perfection, second sight, clairvoyance, extrasensory perception.

Negative: A fanatic, aimless, cynical, pragmatic, a zealot, full of self-superiority.

Repressive: Dishonest, miserly, carnal, insolent.

Number 22—Physical Mastery

Positive: Universal power on the physical level, a financier, a cultured person, capable of international direction in government.

Negative: An inferiority complex, indifferent to mankind, big talker—not doer, an inflated ego.

Repressive: Evil, vicious, crime on a large scale, black magic operator.

Number 33—Emotional Mastery

Positive: The idealistic with power to command or serve, a leader who has emotions under control, constructive controlled ideas.

Negative: Erratic, useless, unemotional, not using his or her gifts of sensitivity to others' emotions, uncaring.

Repressive: Power to work on other people's emotions to their detriment, riot leaders.

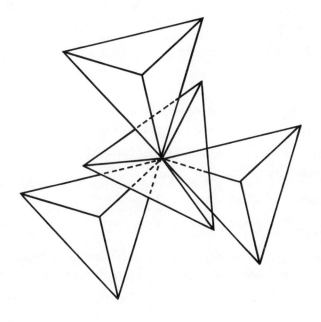

Crystals within crystals,
Pyramids translucent
To reveal
The energies
In your name.

Valeta

Number 44—Mental Mastery

Positive: Universal builder with insight, can institute and assist in reform for the good of mankind, can manifest postulates easily, power on high level of government.

Negative: Mental abilities used to confuse others, twists meanings of great statesmen and very able people in order to use them.

Repressive: Crime through mental cruelty, uses the mask of righteousness to do evil, psychotic.

Number 55—Life Energy

Positive: Abundant life, channels from higher dimensions with ease, brings light into existence, student of action, looks toward future, enthuses others, heals using life force.

Negative: Karma burdened with inaction on the right path, chooses to look backward and wallow in self-pity.

Repressive: Victim of life, no path visible.

Number 66—Love Energy

Positive: Self-realization through love, love extending from self to others, knows that one cannot love others unless he or she knows and recognizes the perfection of one's own soul. This is not an ego trip; this person is full of outpouring love, accepting karma-free relationships in soul. The inner self in deep meditation receives a vision of perfection and yearns for a love relationship with the soul mate as well as the Supreme Being.

Negative: Uses love as a tool to enslave another ("if you loved me you would do whatever I want you to do!"). Extreme selfishness and possessiveness. Refuses love.

Repressive: Sees only the barriers to love; represses loving attention to others, represses the need to outpour cosmic love to others.

Problems Expressing Numbers

If you have a *Master Number* and are not expressing this vibration,
look at the vibration when it is reduced to the single digit:

$$11 = 1 + 1 = 2$$
$$22 = 2 + 2 = 4$$
$$33 = 3 + 3 = 6$$
$$44 = 4 + 4 = 8$$
$$55 = 5 + 5 = 10 = 1$$
$$66 = 6 + 6 = 12 = 3$$

Some people who are totally unaware of their potential could be
expressing the **opposite** side of the numbers. This is different from
the negative side—it is more apathetic. They could be unseeing and
uncaring about what's happening in the world—just plodding along,
doing a job, accepting whatever has to be done. These people are apt
to say, "Well, that's just the way it is and I can't change anything."
They seem to be happy where they are, doing no particular harm,
letting others guide them. When this occurs in a numeroscope, you
may want to suggest some reading material that may help them
become more involved in life.

4
How to Compute Your Birth Name

Before you compute your own birth name, let's use an example chart (Carla Ann Rush) to see how the procedure is done. Chart 1 on page 22 shows us Carla's name and the basic interpretation of her numbers. In order to understand how you compute the vowels, you will need to look at Table 4. We use a special system of number values for each letter, for we work with more Master Numbers than most numerologists.

We have found that A, C, K, V, X, and Z can be used as Master Numbers (and letters). They are interchangeable with their value as a single digit. For instance, K has a value of 11/2; Z has a value of 44/8; C has a value of 66/3; A has a value of 55/1. We always look for the highest value when interpreting a chart in order to discover hidden talents, abilities, attitudes, etc., that may have been overlooked prior to this Aquarian Age we live in.

Each name is divided into three segments as follows:

1) Vowels: A E I O U and sometimes Y or W* = Desire

---

*Y becomes a vowel if there are no other vowels in the syllable. W becomes a vowel when preceded by another vowel.

2) Consonants: the other 20 letters = Dormant self

3) Total Number Value: all the letters = Abilities.

Carla's Chart

In Chart 1 on page 22* we have written in the name CARLA ANN RUSH. The first thing we do is add the vowels in her name. Above her name are blank spaces, and in her chart you will see that 55/1, 55/1, 55/1 and 3 have been written in *above* her name. These are the values of the vowels in Carla's first, middle and last names.

The next thing we do is determine the value of her consonants. Below her name you will see that we wrote in 66/3 for C, 9 for R, 3 for L, 5 for N, 5 for N, 9 for R, 1 for S, and 8 for H. These are all the consonants in her name.

In order to obtain Carla's Desire number we must add up all her vowels. To obtain this number you add the totals of the vowels in her three names. The vowel value of her first name is 110/2; her middle name is 55/10/1 and her last name is 3. If you work with the larger number, you will add 110, 55, and 3 to obtain 15. Then 1 + 5 (or 15) = 6. In our chart we have written 168/15/6, but in your own chart you would only carry the 6 because that is the number you will be working with to interpret her desire number.

To obtain Carla's Dormant Self number, we add the consonants in her name. Her first name equals 78/15/6, her middle name equals 10/1 and her last name is 18/9 for consonant values. When you add these numbers together you get 106, or 16, which equals 7. Again, we have included all the numbers in the chart, but you would only include

---

* Carla's chart (and the chart blanks we have included so you can compute your own numbers) have been done on a modified Numeroscope Form that we use in our practice. The unmodified chart blank contains special categories that require more advanced study so that you can interpret your timing, which we don't go into in this book. We have written a book called *Timing*, which you can buy directly from us. Please write to us in care of F.A.C.E. Association (address in the frontmatter of this book), for details.

Table 4. The Rice System of Number Values

1	2	3	4	5	6	7	8	9	11	22	33	44	55	66
(A)	B	(C)	D	E	F	G	H	I					A	C
J	(K)	L	M	N	O	P	Q	R	K					
S	T	U	(V)	W	(X)	Y	(Z)			V	X	Z		

the 7 if you were doing this for yourself, as the Dormant Self number is 7.

The Abilities number is obtained by adding up both the vowels and the consonants. In order to do this, you move all the numbers to the bottom line of the chart. This line is marked total. This requires that we move the consonant and vowel numbers down to one line. In Carla's first name, the numbers would read 66/3 for C, 55/1 for A, 9 for R, 3 for L, 55/1 for A. You would move the numbers for her middle and last name as well. Now you add the numbers. Her first name adds up to 188/17/8. Her middle name equals 65/11/2 and her last name equals 21/3. In order to add the name, you would simply add up the numbers in her first name ($188 = 1 + 8 + 8 = 17; 1 + 7 = 8$). We have entered all the numbers in the addition process, but if you were doing a numeroscope, you would only add the number 8 to the Abilities section.

If we were to interpret Carla's chart, we would look first to her Desire, Dormant-Self, and Abilities numbers. When we understand the basic interpretation, then we can look to see how the interpretation would vary by using her "expanded numbers."

Desire (Vowels) = 6. Carla's motivation is to create harmony within herself and in her relationships with others. She is able to evaluate character and assist others to make adjustments in their lives by using her natural intuitive ability.

Dormant-Self (Consonants) = 7. Her inner self requires privacy, so she can delve deeper into the mysteries of metaphysics and similar studies. Many will come to her to learn as she learns.

Name ___ Carla Ann Rush ___   Birthdate ___

	110/2	55/1	55/10/1	3						DESIRE 168/15/6	
		55/1		3							Vowels
	C A R L A	A N N	R U S H								Name
44/3	9 3	5 5	9 1 8								Consonants
	78/15/6	10/1	18/9							DORMANT SELF 106/16/7	
44/3	55/1 9 3	55/1 5 5	9 3 1 8								Total
188/17/8		45/4/2	21/3							ABILITIES 274/23/4	

INCLUSION TABLE

1			
2			
3			
4			
5			
6			
7			
8			
9			

KARMA NUMBERS | | |

INTENSIFICATION NUMBERS | | |

PLANES OF EXPRESSION

Mental	Physical	Emotional	Intuitional	
				Inspired
				Dual
				Balanced

FIRST VOWEL _____ CORNERSTONE _____ KEY NUMBER _____

Chart 1. Carla Ann Rush

Abilities (Total number value) = **4**. Carla can accomplish anything that she sets her mind and inner self to do. She can be anything that she wishes as she has the ability to analyze (Dormant self **7**) and set her goals above the ordinary expectations. Success in many fields is available to her (**22**).

If we look at Carla's numbers with the expanded interpretation, we would add the following qualities:

Desire = **15/6**. Carla's creative (**1**) mind can see several pathways (**5**) at once before making decision to move in concert with her co-workers (**6**).

Dormant Self = **16/7**. Her inner self feels this creative (**1**) force moving harmoniously (**6**) to delve more deeply into understanding herself and others (**7**).

Abilities = **22/4**. The gentle 2's (**22**) are harnessed to the practical vibrations of the Master Number **22**. The **4** is organization in the higher echelons of the business world when it is coupled with the Master number **22**. Carla is the dreamer (**2**) who can bring her plans to fruition if she remains practical (**22**) and organized (**4**).

This brief interpretation can be expanded by reading and thinking about the interpretations of the numbers in Carla's name. These numbers are found under the headings Desire, Dormant-Self, and Abilities. We have not discussed the negative side of Carla's numbers. You can look these up. The following pages will discuss how to work out an interpretation more fully.

Computing Desire, Dormant Self and Abilities Numbers

We have worked with Carla's chart as an example, and here is a review list for you to follow when computing your own name. We have included a blank chart (see page 24) so you can work with your own name. Please note that we have also included more blank charts at the back of the book.

Name _____ Birthdate _____

							DESIRE 151/34/7	
84/12/3		69/15/6		16/7				Vowels
5 6		9 55/1	5	5	6	5		Name
L E O N A		D I A N E		E L S T O N E				Consonants
3		5 4	5	3	1 2	5		

DORMANT SELF 28/10 / 1

								Total
8		9		11/2				
3 5 6 5		4 9 55/1 5 5		5 3 1 2 6 5 5				
55/20/2		55/24/6		27/9				

ABILITIES 179/44/8

KARMA
NUMBERS

INTENSIFICATION
NUMBERS

PLANES OF EXPRESSION

	Mental	Physical	Emotional	Intuitional	
					Inspired
					Dual
					Balanced

INCLUSION TABLE

1			
2			
3			
4			
5			
6			
7			
8			
9			

FIRST VOWEL _____ CORNERSTONE _____ KEY NUMBER _____

(your name)

Chart 2

We use the Numerology Fadic system of reducing any triple or double set of numbers to a single digit by adding them horizontally, yet we have kept the entire set of numbers.

If you have no middle name, use the vowels from your first name (or names) and the consonants from your last name (or names) for desire and dormant self. Add the two together for abilities. Double numbers, such as the Master Numbers and the interpretive combinations, provide a connective appraisal or approach to the single digits.

1) Add the value of the vowels for your first name and place the numbers above the first name in the blank space provided on the chart. Repeat for your second (or middle) name, and for your last name.

2) Add the value of the consonants for the first name, the second name and the last name as you did before, placing each set of numbers *below* the names in the blank space provided.

3) Add the sum of the vowels for each name and place this set of numbers in the box to the right after the word **desire**.

4) Add the sum of the consonants for each name and place this set of numbers in the box to the right, after the words **dormant self**.

5) Bring down the numbers from the vowels and the consonants and enter them in the total column. Add these numbers separately for the first, second, and last name, placing the sum of each name in the blank space below.

6) Add the sum of the abilities for each name and place this set of numbers in the box to the right, after the word **abilities**.

Expanded Numbers

We said before that we use the highest numbers to see what may be influencing a person from below the surface. When you look at Carla's chart, you will see a regular interpretation of her numbers—**6** for Desire, **7** for Dormant Self, and **4** for Abilities. In order to recognize the expanded or deeper interpretation, note that we have written on the chart **15/6** for Desire; **16/7** for Dormant Self, and **22/4** for Abilities. You would look at the larger numbers to get the inner interpretation. For example **1** + **5** create a **6**. You may want to go through the tables that follow to determine how this symbolism works. It will be especially insightful when you do your own chart. By looking at Carla's chart, you will see that we have "found" a hidden Master Number by adding 17 + 2 + 3 out of sequence in the Abilities row. This gives us **22**. We always try to "play" with the numbers in this way to see if they will yield a Master Number. Playing with the numbers allows you to discover deeper levels of meaning in your name.

Desire Numbers

The following list of numbers indicates a basic interpretation of how your desire number may manifest. Each desire number has a positive and a negative manifestation. We have also included the color that relates to this number, as well as an interpretation of how the Mars energy will be activated for you.

Desire Number 1

You are independent and want to dominate any situation since you are happiest when in control. People are attracted to you because of your ability to control. Number **1** is always the the color *red* of fire, the vibration of stimulating ideas, stirring the latent fires of imagination in yourself and those around you. This number walks where fools fear to tread, for you are not afraid to experiment with new ideas, people, or relationships. The unusual and exotic entice as you move creatively into the future with unusual concepts. You may find it difficult to accept ideas coming from others in your calculations. Number **1** has a natural urge for independence which can bring great accomplishment. When this energy is not used well, frustration may result, especially if you cannot get others to follow your plans or accept your ideas. You work best alone or in situations where you command others to carry out your wishes exactly. You can handle the main issues of any program by yourself, and you also have the ability to delegate authority, enthusing your staff with your adventurous attitude toward the future.

Mars Energy: This energy carries number **1** forward, in spite of all obstacles, as long as they perform on the positive side of the number. These quick minds and active intelligences are happiest when busy with many projects. No matter what sign your Mars is in, you will be a go-getter.

Color: Red

Negative 1: Needs to cultivate friendliness and acquire interest in others. Attention to other people and their vibrations can bring more success to your plans and adventures. You need to curb impatience. Listen to some opinions other than your own, and you will make better choices as far as your goals in life are concerned.

Desire Number 2

You want and need a peaceful existence, surrounded by your family, friends and a loving atmosphere. Your friendliness attracts marriage and business partners since you make your space so comfortable and harmonious. You are kind and thoughtful—a natural peacemaker. You are sensitive to your own feelings as well as those of others. It's easy for you to fall in love and you can form a good partnership via marriage as you are willing to compromise your feelings for your mate.

In business or political partnerships, you can become the diplomat who smooths the way for the leaders of society or of the world. Your love of peace can lead others out of chaos.

Number **2** desires to oil the wheels of commerce, avoiding arguments by suggesting proper action in a gentle way that gracefully leads combatants to a peaceful settlement of differences.

Mars Energy: The Mars fire is "banked," for the energy does not burn brisk and hot, it has been carefully prepared to last the night. This energy produces a warm glow that attracts others, for they want to snuggle up to warm egos and themselves. No matter what sign your Mars is in, the quality of carefulness will be added to it.

Color: Orange—Number 2 uses the earthy energy of persuasiveness for healing. This color calms the emotions much like water soothes the fevered brow.

Negative 2: Your constancy and devotion to detail can be annoying to those who have a different goal. Number 2 needs to strengthen the life purpose as you are apt to vacillate in your desire to please others. You can become overly sensitive emotionally, or so interested in keeping the peace, that others may feel you are a weakling and may try to push you in a direction you don't want to pursue. Number 2 has a limit to patience and may scratch like a cornered cat. At the lowest level, 2's pressured unfairly may become hostile and sweetly ruin the person pressuring them.

Desire Number 3

You are eternally seeking happiness and perfection on all planes, scattering sunshine, love, and beauty on all who come into your realm. You enjoy the social side of life, such as entertaining, performing, or appreciating art and music. It is easy to acquire knowledge, for you prefer to work from inspiration and intuition while ignoring ritual. When mistakes occur in business, you may be temporarily upset, venting your frustrations on the nearest object or person. Before long you pick yourself up and start over again, knowing that the future will bring more action, entertainment, or bigger and better business deals. If you have an unfulfilling emotional relationship, you cannot understand how someone can't understand you. In relationships you may think that you are communicating clearly, when in fact you are not. When you are hurt in emotional relationships, you may become upset and rant and rave about how you helped "so-and-so" and you got nothing in return. This may happen when you give of yourself freely and expect others to respond to you emotionally. It might be wise to look before you leap.

Mars Energy: Mars glows for Number 3, producing sparks that touch and enthuse those around you. Enthusiasm is a quality that will be added to any sign your Mars is in.

Color: Yellow—like sunshine—brings warmth and shines on many. Yellow is the sparkle and energy brought by the sun.

Negative 3: Guard against over-reacting. You may take the spotlight from others or invalidate other people's talents. You can dim your image with wastefulness and conceit. You may need to cultivate patience, for you move quickly from one thing to another, and you may miss some of the road signs along the way. Concentration may be short or you get bored easily.

Desire Number 4

You seek respectability—the esteem of your peers and friends. You are willing to deny yourself (and sometimes others) in order to maintain order and uphold your concept of tradition. You love your home, country, and revere your flag. You respect authority and tend to respond to situations in a more traditional manner, rather than improvising. You gain personal satisfaction from being thorough and correct on the job or in your behavior. You expect loyalty from your co-workers and demand perfection from them as well as yourself. Most people respect you for this viewpoint as they feel they can trust your judgment. Lasting friendships are more important to you than a long list of casual relationships. You have few trusted friends but they know where your loyalties are and respect you for this. You often repel love although you want and need more than the average person.

Mars Energy: A steady flame that glows in dark places for those who seek the light. No matter what sign your Mars is in, your action will be steady and firm.

Color: Green—the healing color of earth's plants. This soothing color is a panacea for our mortal tired visions.

Negative 4: You can be rigid, opinionated and unwilling to unbend your self-righteous attitudes. You may be very tight with money, not

realizing that the outflow and inflow of money (spending and earn-
ing) increases your prosperity. Number **4** expects perfection in
others, being extremely selective when picking friends. This expecta-
tion can be disappointing as no one is perfect. Have you looked at
yourself? Are you perfect? Do you project your imperfections on your
friends?

Desire Number 5

You desire personal freedom, requiring a lot of change and variety in
both your profession and personal life. You welcome new opportunities with eagerness so you can learn more about life. You would rather
learn from experience than study with an authority. This number
symbolizes the traveler, whether you travel physically or mentally.
You seek adventure, looking for release from drudgery and detail.
You can be at home in any country, gathering, or class as you
contribute warmth and exuberance. You can take conventional ideas
and twist them slightly so you learn more than is apparent to the casual
viewer. The motivation of **5** is using the creative mind on the mental
level, creating things (material objects as well as ideas). You can be a
wonderful lover but you move from one person to another, experiencing change instead of constancy.

Mars Energy: This is a radiant energy, and you are capable of
brushing others with butterfly wings full of ideas. No matter what
your Mars sign is, you will add to it the quality of enthusiasm.

Color: Turquoise—a refreshing blend of green for healing and blue
for the sky.

Negative 5: The impulsive and seemingly short-sighted moves or
decisions that you make could give others the impression that you are
irresponsible. Carelessness and self-indulgence could certainly bring
about abuse of your freedom instead of setting you free. If you start
more projects than you can finish and have many of these unfinished
cycles hanging over your head like Damocles' sword, you could
become inconsistent with your true purpose in life—which is to bring
change that is useful and good. Also, no empathy for others, or

over-indulgence in food, dope, or drink can bring your motivations to a low ebb.

Desire Number 6

You desire harmonious relationships with your family, friends, and associates. Your principle aim is to create this harmony, balancing the chaos around you with humor and understanding. Beauty and comfort attract the best in you—whether it be in your home or in places of pleasure, such as concerts, movies, plays or dancing. The colors you choose for your home or office express your fine feelings for texture, shape and balance. You prefer to work with others rather than by yourself. You provide clean, clear space for your co-workers to express themselves, their problems and their desires. The comfort you give to others is rare. Technically you are not the peacemaker, but your deep understanding can provide a resting place for troubled people. You provide tranquility that others need in order to solve their personal or business problems.

Mars Energy: Courage is demonstrated in the **6**. Your courage is backed by a vitality that overcomes the hurts of the world or those of close relationships. No matter what sign your Mars is in at birth, you will act with courage.

Color: Royal blue—indicating stability. This deep blue radiates healing and tranquility. The royal part of the color indicates the confidence that is required to take charge of any distress that may occur around you.

Negative 6: Although you can take care of other people's problems, you may become so efficient at this that you begin to interfere. The anxiety that you are apt to express in moments of stress can create chaos instead of balancing the chaos with a calm detached manner. Another negative aspect of **6** is carelessness. You leave jobs undone, don't finish cycles of work or ideas and eventually get to the point where emotions are highly charged. This can then turn into a cynical attitude or domestic tyranny.

Desire Number 7

Your search for knowledge and wisdom leads you into strange corridors as you willingly venture into investigations of the unknown. Because of a need to dissect the philosophies of life many people do not understand you. Although they do not comprehend how you arrived at the answers, they recognize your depth of reasoning and trust your analytical approach to both abstract and concrete problems. When people can penetrate your reserve and reluctance to discuss details they learn to love and trust your judgment. You prefer to attract people to you rather than force their attention. This impression of remoteness lends authority to the times when you are willing to communicate. Your deliberate choice of words reflects a person who thinks deeply or who is thinking on several levels at one time. Number 7 is the kind and gentle lover who wants affection, but who is unsure of how to communicate this to a partner. You could be an interesting mate as no one is ever sure of what you are thinking or planning.

Mars Energy: Here Mars works like a laser beam that cuts through the dross, hitting the target exactly. Many may miss the altered state of consciousness of your energy. No matter what sign your Mars is in, this "sureness" will be added to the other qualities symbolized by your Mars.

Color: Violet—indicating reverence for things mystical. This is the bridge over the water of change from mundane to esoteric.

Negative 7: The fear of showing emotion causes 7's to withdraw into themselves in order to avoid being hurt. Since you usually prefer to work things out alone you seem aloof from the madding crowd. Too much random behavior around you causes confusion. At the lowest level of expression you can be malicious; you may cheat to win, or become suppressive to self and others.

Desire Number 8

Your paramount desire is for power and control over others as you are ambitious for material success. Money is very important to you—lots of it—for you know the power money holds. This power and control does not need to express itself negatively. On the positive side **8** is the desire to manage and direct others for **8** knows how to organize and finance big business. Your ideas are expansive and cover the overview instead of the minute details (which **2**'s handle very well). Your courage and industry motivate you to move forward, and you use tremendous energy to inspire people to greater efforts to accomplish the tasks you propose. You can be a tremendous power for good, showing others how to gain prosperity (money, goods, or metaphysical prosperity). As an executive you are sure of the steps necessary to achieve your goals. At the same time you can delegate authority to others, leaving them in charge of affairs with scant supervision, as you expect loyalty from peers and employees. You usually receive loyalty from those you govern as you also understand the responsibilities of power.

Mars Energy: A direct blue flame hovers above the material candle of physical life. It is the impetus that provides the heat for your endeavor and accomplishment. Industry and control are qualities that are added to your natal Mars.

Color: Rose—the color of love, the expression of the power of love to move partners with passion.

Negative 8: Sometimes you are so busy charging ahead with plans and propositions that patience wears thin when you need to deal with other numbers (such as the analytical **7** or the detailed energy of **2**). Pay attention to the less efficient peers to make relationships glide a little smoother. You can be intolerant of slower minded people. Your biased viewpoint can become abusive and unjust and your weakest way of expressing yourself is playing the bigot.

Desire Number 9

Your motivation is to serve mankind with love and sympathetic understanding. You are ready to sublimate yourself and your desires in order to serve the whole world. You broadcast your energies and your talents without giving a thought to your own impoverishment. Since you desire to do so many things for others, you tend to think of them first and yourself last, expending your energies in many directions and being careless of your own goals. Your message and your interpretation of the great benefits to all will endear you to many. This broad viewpoint and your intuition will lead you to advanced concepts in the humanities. The positive side of this humanitarian number can touch a responsive cord of recognition in many people. As this cord vibrates the energy transcends bias and prejudice against other belief systems and races, assisting individuals and countries to understand each other. Here is the romantic—the faithful, loyal suitor who brings flowers to compliment the beloved. Number **9** may not be as constant as the **4**. They become absorbed in projects, however, when they are ready, they are attentive lovers wanting and needing personal as well as universal love.

Mars Energy: Here the Mars energy is like the rosy light of dawn breaking over a sea of compassion. The natural tendencies indicated by your natal Mars will be colored by an ability to act with compassion.

Color: Yellow-gold—the glow of perfection in the humanities.

Negative 9: Needs to balance desire energies. The flow of love becomes so strong that you need to express devotion to constituents which could "turn off" your peers. This expression could be grossly misunderstood and judged very harshly by unenlightened souls. You might rush forward with ideals, ignoring common sense, as you get sentimentally involved with issues. This indiscretion could turn to bitterness and immorality.

Desire Number 11

You are an uncompromising idealist who desires perfected vision through psychic and extrasensory powers. You are more concerned with aesthetic spiritual values than practical logic (shown by **4**). Your great interior strength wants to create an ideal future. You love ideals more than the individual, and desire to communicate these inspirations to groups. Your passion is seeking salvation for mankind rather than a single person. You insist upon what is right (as you see it) regardless of the human condition. You seek a direct line to the highest universal vibrations for your reformation projects. Truth and beauty are paramount in your desire for perfection. You need at least two creative outlets at one time, and are constantly striving to fulfill both. You are the lover who demands (and gets) soft music, candle-light, fine wine and no interruptions to the flow of lovemaking. The fine tuning of **11** can come crashing to a halt with the ringing of the phone or doorbell.

Mars Energy: Inspiring bursts of zealous endeavor. Therefore zealousness will be added to the natural tendencies of your natal Mars.

Color: Silver—the color of **11** attracts others, magnetizing the de-sired person to your side with hypnotic energy.

Negative 11: This Master Number (reducible to a **2**) can bring conflict between the idealistic nature (**11**) and the need to be a peacemaker at all costs (**2**). If **11**'s vacillate in this manner they can become aimless in their motivations, wasting their spiritual excellence. Here you will find the fanatic who feels superior to his or her peers, the zealot who rides roughshod over any other idea or ideal which is contrary to his or her plans. This superior attitude can degenerate into a cynical approach to relationships and insolent distrust of others. The Master Numbers carry a great deal of responsibility for the bearer.

Desire Number 22

You are a person who will promote freedom and progress along practical lines. Your executive abilities will carry you into building now and for the future. Since you are a practical person, your ideas will be based on solid facts, efficiently carried through to their final completion. This master number gives you the vibration of the dreamer but you are harnessed to a vibration that requires you to have plans that are useful and sensible. The perfect world for you contains feasible designs to assist others to realize their dreams. You can be trusted, for you love people. The tremendous plans you conceive can have extraordinary results, since you personally apply your expertise to achieve the results you imagined in your wakening dreams. Your love life yields to romance, dinner at the finest of restaurants, theatre, expensive gifts to your loved one, gifts that also are useable. Your mate needs to accept your mastery and the kind of superpower that you have if he or she is to stay near your vibration.

Mars Energy: Like a brush fire, it ignites the energies of those around you. This practical energy for action will be added to the natural tendencies of your natal Mars.

Color: Red-gold—denotes practical wisdom which can be used to clean away the soil of unclean action.

Negative 22: With all this awesome ability comes *responsibility* for your actions. Negative actions can destroy the very things you wish to accomplish. Your intelligence cannot be boxed, it needs fresh air and exposure to many viewpoints in order to work on a broader base than a **4**, for **4**'s have a limited vista of imagination compared to **22**. If you cannot follow through with your grandiose plans you can become a "big-talker" with a get-rich-quick scheme. On the lowest level of vibration you may become involved with crime or black magic.

Desire Number 33

With diligence and study you can become master of your emotions, understanding the emotions people exhibit under certain circumstances. You have the intelligence to decipher and use emotions to your greatest advantage without hurting anyone providing you stay on the positive side of the number. You work through your feelings, both your own and others, understanding other's emotions to bring about agreements of a huge scale. This is useful and valuable when bringing two parties, two political factions, or two countries to an agreement. You are able to bring these opposite poles of personal or national dictum together for reasonable discussion. Your grasp of the totality of the case in point (and the high feeling engendered by the lower emotions of the persons involved) can bring the solution to the problem as long as your desire is to bring peace. You are the highly motivated emotional lovers who rollercoast from ecstatic raptures to the pitfalls of self-denial and self-punishment. The master number **33** is a combination of **22** (the double peacemaker) combined with the genius of **11**.

Mars Energy: Glitters like tiny solar cells giving off twinkling light to receptive persons. No matter what sign your Mars is in, you will add compassion and emotional depth to your actions.

Color: Deep sky-blue—for intensity. The sky and water can cool highly charged emotions.

Negative 33: You can be totally unemotional about using your power of control, erratic about control, or you can fall into the trap of controlling others through their emotions. This vibration has the power to work on other people's emotions to bring them into servitude and keep them there through fear. You can also be trapped by others who dramatize their emotions.

Desire Number 44

This genius level of practicality works in two worlds, the physical and the mental. These people can manifest whatever they want on this planet—cars, food, money, glory, fame, friends and just about anything that they desire. This is the mental master. In this number is the beginning of form. Number **1** is the creative principle; number **2** is the container that holds the creation temporarily; number **3** is the movement in the container; and number **4** is the beginning of form as resistance comes into being. This double **4** (**44**) has extraordinary powers of concentration, emotional balance, and the ability to practically apply any of those things he or she wishes to manifest in the outer world. These structures could be something in form, something that can be seen or touched, or they can be visions of ideas (**11**) which **44** can put into practical form. Inherent in **44** is the idealism of **11**, the logic approach of **22**, the emotional mastery of **33**. This form of love takes on a healing quality for those who come in contact with **44**. She or he can dissect a problem, and by using a calm, rational approach can reach the condition of the person so they can see clearly through the problem.

Mars Energy: Scintillates with contained potency characteristic of the crystal as it rotates in the sunlight of understanding. Crystal clarity will be added to the natural tendencies of the sign of your Mars.

Color: Deep blue-green—tranquilizing is the color for **44**. This beautiful earth color radiates from **44** when she or he is at the highest point of vibration.

Negative 44: The amount of power in **44** can be difficult to handle and turns into a degraded situation when **44** uses this vibration to attain desires at any cost. There is an inherent threat of rigidity in the attitude that "I am always right because I am always right," that could send **44** into spasms of confusion. Here is crime through mental cruelty or the use of the mask of righteousness to do evil.

Desire Number 55

This number is the expression of life after form is completed. It is like creating a statue—putting the clay into the mold, shaking the mold and after a proper length of time a solid form is produced. It may be beautiful but it may also be lifeless. Then **55** comes along and energizes the form and we have something that contains a life force. Number **55** symbolizes the abundance of life, the joyful voice of delight and happiness, the desire to fly higher than anyone has gone before. When a **55** walks into a room it seems to light up and people are attracted to this radiance. Number **55** can learn to be a channel for higher beings by quieting himself and letting this white light come through for **55** acts like a prism, breaking the white into rainbows of color. What a joy to make love with this exuberant, joy filled person!

Mars Energy: Symbolizes newly created life as **55** moves around the universe with effervescence. This energy will be added to the natural tendencies of your natal Mars.

Color: Red-violet—the color of life energy. This is a spiritual color that radiates through the air.

Negative 55: This strong vibration is ignored by many since our Master Numbers have not been discovered in this context until now. We have known that each name which reduces to a **1** could hold the possibility of higher powers. If **55**'s reduce anyone's life force by mental cruelty, emotional suppression, invalidation of their logical approach, or scoffing at their idealism (**44, 33, 22,** and **11** all inherent in the **55**) they become burdened with heavy karma in this lifetime. On the lowest vibration they become a victim of life, seeking only darkness, deceit and self-flagellation.

Desire Number 66

This is the master love energy number. This is universal love for all mankind. The motivation for a person holding this number is the potential of being totally self-realized and willing to take the risk of going public to express this vibration of love for all nations and peoples. You have been the keeper of the love flame and you must teach and share your knowledge with others. This is the Yin and the Yang—the female and the male energy coming together to make the whole being. You are being quickened in love to be ready to read the Akashic records. Only a few have passed their initiations, enabling them to read the records as they must be read—with understanding and love—so that no false energy is passed on down through the ages. Number **66** is truly the cosmic mother, the double **6** leads to the nine (or, $6 \times 6 = 36 = 9$) which is brotherly love and the completion of cycles. The potential to leave this earthly plane when you are ready, so you can move forward into the next plane, read the scrolls in the house of scrolls to become enlightened, and attend the Hall of Wisdom on this next plane.

Mars Energy: A ray that touches the soul raising him or her above ordinary love to ecstasy. Universal love will be a factor of expression no matter what sign your Mars is in.

Color: Ultra rose—the fullest expression of love on this plane. Meditation on this color will open the heart chakra fully if all the other laws are followed which have led you to this initiation.

Negative 66: If a person is not at the highest level of this vibration on the positive side he or she can use love as a tool to enslave another. This negative energy can degenerate into repressing loving attention to others and repressing the outpouring of love to others.

Dormant Self Numbers

The following listing indicates a positive and negative interpretation of dormant self numbers. This number relates to the Moon in your birthchart. Even though your Moon could be in any one of twelve signs, and will reflect the energy symbolized by the sign it's in, your Moon will also reflect some of the qualities of the number that signifies your dormant self.

Dormant Self Number 1

This symbolizes the pioneering personality who is unafraid to venture into strange worlds to discover how others think and plan. Number 1's do not necessarily accept other's viewpoints; however, they do explore and think about new avenues, storing this information until it coalesces into a form they can use creatively.

This optimistic personality always sees the interesting side of a project and how it can be improved by starting all over again. Or perhaps they see the project from another dimension than most people see. Their creative mind seeks the unknown and the untried. Their self-determinism forges ahead into strange pathways, as they seek the perfect solution to projects, problems and programs. This creative personality startles others as they scramble to keep up with the sparkle and determination of the **1**'s.

The Moon reflects the courage of **1**'s as they explore the dark places of the mind and spirit. As the Moon shines in the darkest part of the twenty-four hours so does **1** reflect upon the dark corners of hidden, unexplored territory. No matter what your natal Moon sign, you will reflect with a certain kind of optimism.

Negative Expression: When **1**'s are exhibiting their negative side they become indecisive and vacillate between this and that project. Each avenue seems so new and exciting they are unable to choose, so they do nothing as they wait for more and better ideas. Another factor is their arrogance in assuming that they know it all. They refuse to take other's viewpoint, even on an experimental basis. If things do not go their way they may attempt to lie their way out of a situation—very cleverly, of course. And at the lowest expression of their personality, **1**'s become hostile to those around them, bearing ill will for no reason than **1**'s inability to accept other people's opinions at face value.

Dormant Self Number 2

This is the personality that creates peace and a calm atmosphere just by being in the room. These people radiate love for family, in their personal life with mate, children, and relatives, or in their business life which is a created family structure for them as well. They see themselves as caring for others, going quietly in their unassuming way to settle arguments by presenting compromises so that each side can come into agreement without hostility or loss of face.

This personality exhibits the fine points of diplomacy, letting the leaders wave the banners of independence as they (**2**'s) go quietly about oiling the wheels of commerce. Number **2**'s are sensitive to vibrations and can anticipate the needs of another person without having to ask where the problem lies. The inner self responds to love and will protect family or employer from outside negative vibrations as long as the **2** is appreciated.

The Moon's soft light bathes the 2's in tranquility so they can reflect this gentleness to others. Gentleness is a quality that is added to the other characteristics of your Moon sign.

Negative Expression: Number 2's can lose their identity if they sublimate their personality to another. If they take the line of least resistance because they are reluctant to argue for themselves, their peaceful, sensitive personality can be turned inwardly on themselves. This sensitivity to self then becomes the "poor me" syndrome and results in the complainer—the whiner who blames all his or her woes on another. As the 2 continues to act in an impatient way, he or she becomes mischievous. This covertly hostile attitude is the lowest vibration, the "I'm going to get even with you without you knowing what happened!" The 2 needs to learn that he or she can assist others without losing his identity if he remembers he is a peacemaker, a go-between.

Dormant Self Number 3

This is a witty personality with charm to spare. Number 3's are popular with most people because they spread a lot of sunshine wherever they go. When they walk into a room, eyes turn as they radiate warmth and personality that attract people for others want to bask in this glow. Number 3 is full of fun, quick with repartee, telling fascinating stories with a verve, and anecdotes that fascinate the listener. The personality requires an audience and is the happiest when surrounded by admiring people of both sexes. The inner self has an intuitive quality which recognizes the need for laughter and the light touch. Number 3's communicate well, seeing themselves as the entertainers of a group—and they are. They can also communicate with higher beings as they are more open to receiving inspiration than most numbers.

The Moon reflects the interest that 3's have in others as a mirror reflects the true self. The love and humor they bring to every relationship assist others to move away from a dire or heavy "life is serious and grim" attitude that prevails so much in our society.

Negative Expression: Number 3 can become conceited as he sees people reaching out and begins to believe that he is the central sun for mankind. In this conceit they could begin to exaggerate their stories beyond belief and lose their audience. When **3**'s become the dilettante, dabbling and hardly ever looking at where they are or where they're going, they lose their sense of radiance and stability. Then they look for someone to gossip about—someone else in the limelight who seems to be taking their place. They may then become intolerant, jealous or may become judgmental of others.

Dormant Self Number 4

These personalities are devoted to duty, doing the "right" thing; they are loyalty personified, attaching themselves to a person, group or company with unswerving devotion. You can count on them to be prompt with appointments, exact in evaluations, and considerate with others. They are ruled by a cautious inner sense which disturbs their sense of fairness if they are required to lie—even a little "white lie" to save another's feelings. They do not wish to attract attention, preferring to be one of the group. In their reserve they think before speaking, and listen well to your problems without offering suggestions unless they feel you are doing something that may impinge on your personal safety. This orderly self precludes ingenuity but does outline the skilled person who realizes within that flashes of genius belong to others. They make wonderful mates, accepting your affection, although inhibited in their outward expression of love. They make good, stable parents, building a sound structure for nurturing children.

The Moon reflects their devotion and sincerity, and these qualities will be added to whatever sign your Moon is in.

Negative Expression: They have natural feelings toward order which can become inflexible—even turning to rigidity—if allowed to go downtone. They can become stiff, unbending, moral antagonists who stop all communication or refuse to pass on communications if their sense of justice is offended by criticism. They can become plodders if they become negative, just going along not really caring and becoming clumsy in their actions. At the lowest vibrations, they become hateful and vulgar, preferring to suppress people and ideas.

Dormant Self Number 5

These personalities desire personal freedom. They can accept responsibility if authorities will leave them alone so they can make their own decisions at their level of work. If the boss hovers over a 5 he or she is apt to make many more mistakes and get upset at the "closeness" or a closing in of their space. Give 5's instructions, leave them on their own and if they are vibrating on a positive level they will enhance their job—they may think up better ways to get it done. Their inner self knows that the ways of doing and thinking about things are unlimited and they enjoy "changing" a process or material object so that the performance increases productivity. Number 5's have a native understanding of others and can reflect moods and desires. This understanding gives them an inner sense of "timing" which is very valuable for people who contact the public. They know when to close a sale, they know when to be still, when to empathize, when to move on to new adventures.

The Moon reflects your zest for life. Although your natal Moon may be in one of the more serious signs, such as Capricorn, this number will add the quality of zest to your basic Moon expression.

Negative Expression: A rolling stone gathers no moss but does acquire a beautiful shine. This adventurous spirit in 5's can lead to inconsistency in love, or erratic behavior in business. Negative 5's are late to work, sloppy in dress, preferring pleasures to honoring their word or promises. On this level 5's are possessive and inconsiderate of those they profess to love. And yet they expect to be understood and forgiven for their selfish actions. At the lowest level self-indulgence will lead to fear of change and little sympathy for others as they fear getting involved. Freedom is challenged as the self is boxed in until some cataclysmic shock occurs to shake them into seeing the higher side of their personalities.

Dormant Self Number 6

This is the personality of harmony, for **6**'s have a sense of fair play that is recognized by their peers. They propose social reforms to improve the distribution of monies, services and justice. Their reports are carefully worded to advance both sides of the problem in question. Their inner selves want a fair shake for everyone and they will communicate this attitude up or down the line of command. They do not like to take sides, preferring to listen before making decisions to elevate or fire someone in their employ. This does not mean that **6**'s are fence riders, it means that they seek fair play for all. They are the compromisers as they feel that everyone should have a chance to explain their feelings toward whatever problem is at stake. Their compassionate personality sees good in everyone at some level. They are the cosmic comforters who are prone to organize friends and family toward peace, hospitality, and beauty.

The Moon reflects a harmonizing influence as this cool light calms the rushing wind of discontent. A sense of fair play will be added to the natural tendencies symbolized by your Moon sign.

Negative Expression: This intense searching for peace and contentment can lead **6**'s into meddling where they are not wanted. They can disorganize other people's lives if they are not invited to do so. Each number has its own vibration and **6**'s want to calm and equalize each person—a quality that is welcome to many but also shunned by many, especially those who are leaders and have to face many trials. Number **6**'s can become anxious about their family and business associates to the point of tyranny when operating on the negative side of this number. At the lowest vibration, they become cynical and suspicious and hide behind pride and self-righteousness. All this negativity can be stopped if they remember they are the harmonizing influence on this earth.

Dormant Self Number 7

These are studious personalities for **7**'s look to books and authorities to refine their analytical minds. They delve into mysteries of the unknown in order to understand more about how people plan their lives and think about themselves. They are intensely interested in finding out about the games people play on each other. Sometimes they enter the game and get caught in the middle because they are not reluctant to voice opinions! They are seldom bored as they are interested in many subjects, taking an active interest in subjects related to philosophy as well as down to earth projects that require the use of their hands to fashion a solid structure. The inner wisdom inherent in the 7 carries them into the future toward a better life. They spend profitable time alone, being as good company for themselves as with others. This is the number of the mystic, those who delve into metaphysical mysteries. Their emotions run high as they search diligently for the truth. These are the thinkers of the world.

The Moon reflects wisdom and reserve. Wisdom will be added to the natural tendencies symbolized by the sign your Moon is in.

Negative Expression: On the inner planes, too much study without practical application can become confusing to 7's. If one authority refutes another, 7's can become skeptical about the subject they are studying until they sit down to analyze what they have read. Then they can move to the positive side of the number for correct interpretation. With this high emotional content, 7's can get trapped into becoming people who, when backed into a corner, uses humiliation to get even. They are contenders, remaining aloof until attacked either physically or verbally. On the lowest vibration they remain ignorant, becoming malicious, and not above cheating others.

Dormant Self Number 8

This is the personality of success. Number 8's know how to gather and demonstrate power to others as well as for themselves. They know how to get things done as efficiently as possible in the shortest time and expect others to do the same. They see themselves as heads of large corporations, controlling sizable interests, lives and destinies. They are exacting and determined that their work and philosophy be the best. They expect the same diligence from their employees and their co-workers. They command respect and get it for they are valuable to themselves and to others. On the mystical side, 8's can reach high, for this is the inner number of the possibility of the opening of the third eye—the all seeing eye that can discover the hidden vibrations of others and use this discovery for the benefit of mankind. This active, cheerful person inspires others to do their best.

The Moon reflects courage, determination and fairness. These traits will be added to those that are evident from your Moon sign.

Negative Expression: If **8**'s become too bossy or arrogant, they begin to lose their power and prestige. As this loss continues they can become intolerant of others, blaming others for their own mistakes. If they become infatuated with the love of power, they can reduce their inner strength by scheming to get more and more, not knowing that more is never enough. Another negative manifestation of this number indicates an inability to handle money, lack of ambition, lack of love or caring for others. On the lowest vibration, **8**'s become abusive in act and language because they feel inwardly that they are just showing the weakness of the oppressor.

Dormant Self Number 9

This is the personality of brotherhood to all mankind. Number **9**'s feel responsible to humanity and express this in an eagerness to serve others in any way which will progress mankind toward higher goals. They feel an evangelical purpose to lead others out of the wilderness of chaotic belief systems. Their zeal is coupled with quiet and intense leadership that persuades rather than forces. They may seem to be spectators in life for they discuss issues and quietly presenting ideals to consider rather than presenting a brute attack. Their inner selves want personal love as well as impersonal compassion. They are romantics and see themselves in this role when they are fantasizing. This type of personality contributes to success as they are willing to listen to the woes of others. They offer assistance to employees and co-workers because they don't like to see others trapped in emotional or financial binds.

The Moon reflects brotherhood to all mankind. Responsibility will color the natural tendencies symbolized by your Moon sign.

Negative Expression: They need to remember their intense need to "save" people can become a judgment. It implies that those less fortunate need to come up to **9**'s standards. They can become scornful of "lesser" or "downtrodden" persons if their negative unforgiving nature is uppermost. Another emotion that **9**'s need to guard against is the impulse to give and give without accepting something sincerely offered in return. This compulsion to always give and never receive stems from the fear of not being good enough "no matter what you do." This "giving excessively" is something to watch in a negative **9** in business as he or she may give everything away. At the lowest vibration, **9**'s feel bitter and cannot understand why they are unsuccessful when actually they are stopping the inflow of love by not accepting it.

Dormant Self Number 11

This is the personality of faith. Number **11** sees themselves as messengers going into the world to teach the truth to humanity and guide people into the spiritual path of faith. They seek to reform people by assisting them to see and understand the principles of life and living. Their faith in themselves is untouchable, and when **11**'s are by themselves they see clearly what must be done in order to bring clarity to the comprehension of others. They see themselves as the harbinger of new ways to dissect words and thoughts. They dream of a world of enlightened people. Their inspiration is to change the attitudes of others and channel them into growth patterns, enabling people to break the chains which surround our accepted norms.

The Moon reflects sincere striving for the fulfillment of a dream or a perfect world. Faith is a characteristic that will be added to your Moon sign.

Negative Expression: With all this positive faith **11**'s see in themselves, it would seem difficult to ever imagine that they could operate on the negative side of the number eleven. One of the tests that **11**'s must face is learning to use their tremendous talents, reducing aimlessness and getting "with it" to expand their dreaming into actual "doing." Many times they feel reluctant to impart their inner knowledge. This reluctance can degenerate into a cynical attitude as they become frustrated with established thinking patterns of our planet. The lowest vibration of **11**'s is dishonesty—with themselves and others—they fear being exposed as true thinkers.

Dormant Self Number 22

This is the personality of physical mastery. Number **22**'s see themselves as understanding physical laws and applying them with reason and logic. They dream of a perfect construction (when they take time out to dream, as they are usually very busy). They see themselves as the master planners in industry, government, philanthropic ventures and humanitarian activities. The keyword here is action. They have brought with them the self-determinism to plan and execute their dream in concrete, steel and law.

They see themselves rewarded in material goods for their efforts in incorporating empires of vast import, while being loved, respected, and depended upon by family and close friends. Negative blows and unexpected hardships can be turned into an asset by **22**'s providing they are expressing the positive side of this Master Number. This powerful inner self can literally move mountains to achieve the success they rightfully believe is physically possible.

The Moon reflects an ability to concentrate on building a secure world through an innate diplomatic approach. Diplomacy is a trait that will be added to the natural qualities symbolized by your Moon sign.

Negative Expression: The magnificent plans and dreams of **22**'s need to be acted upon; if they only talk a good story while living in their imaginations, they will never rise to their impressive height. If **22**'s become negative in moments of stress, they may blame others for inefficiency, as their inflated egos cannot permit fault in themselves. There are times when they become indifferent to employees and co-workers. Some **22**'s exhibit an inferiority complex, having no faith in themselves.

Dormant Self Number 33

These personalities are idealists who are masters of their emotions—emotional masters. The power to command others by triggering their emotions is power, indeed, and must not be abused. Number 33's can fall harder and with more destruction than a 6.

If a 33 has ever wondered why they were different than family and friends, learning they are a 33 could help them understand why. Their idealistic pursuits can be accomplished—no matter what. Friends (?) may try to stop 33's from accomplishing goals because they are not vibrating to the same rhythm. Number 33's move fast and can juggle more than one emotion at one time. They need to learn the rhythm of their emotions and understand them as well as they can, for this is a valuable gift if used correctly.

The Moon reflects intensity and emotional drive. These qualities will be added to those symbolized by the sign your Moon is in.

Negative Expression: Controlling the emotions does not mean suppressing them. It means understanding the positive and the negative vibrations of the scale of the emotions from a low "I don't care attitude," through grief, anger, up to and including emotions such as being interested and enthusiastic about whatever. Number 33's can lose these gifts of evaluation if they begin to exhibit an unfeeling attitude for others.

On the negative side confusion and chaotic situations can produce erratic decisions.

If 33's are not using these gifts they can become unemotional and non-caring about a job or human relationships. The lowest emotional expression uses the power to work on other people's emotions to their detriment. Leaders of riots, people who disrupt the orderly function of society can be 33's who don't function at their best.

Dormant Self Number 44

This is the personality of mental mastery. Number 44's can control both factions of disagreeing parties and settle differences by analyzing both sides of the disagreement. They are not necessarily interested in the emotional side of the arguments; they search for facts, questioning people, and relate one fact to another for reference to bring both parties together for conferences. This is not the peacemaker and appeaser. Number **44**'s are diligent in their study of world situations; they gather information. The positive expression of this number has control and understanding of themselves. They see themselves using these gifts in high levels of government, corporations or by performing services in a spiritual way. The cool exterior that **44**'s exhibit is misleading to many as it looks like indifference, when it is an inner knowingness rather than a "cool" facade. Number **44**'s see themselves shedding bright light on the hidden issues that need to see the light of day.

The Moon reflects mental healing qualities. Healing others will be a natural tendency and will combine with the other traits symbolized by your Moon sign.

Negative Expression: The higher we go in Master Numbers the lower we can fall if we turn to the negative side. If **44**'s twist information in order to gain an advantage over opponents, they will be denying their great gifts of mental power. They could use this power to create confusion in the lives of other people, thereby creating confusion in their own lives and destroying their ability to think clearly and quickly. The lowest vibration of **44** is crime through mental cruelty, using the mask of righteousness. When **44**'s really slide downhill they become psychotic.

Dormant Self Number 55

This personality expresses abundant life. Number **55**'s can channel from higher beings or dimensions with ease if they are vibrating on the positive side of this number. They have life energy, spreading light and exuberance to all who come within their range. They have a powerful life force, and hold the secret of how to increase the life flow for themselves and for others.

Their inner selves know that the Father gives unstintingly to His children and may wonder why others do not see this and bask in the wondrous glow. They believe in spiritual healing through love and serenity of being. This belief is imparted to all who come within range of their powerful aura. As the song says, "This is the sunshine of our lives."

Our solar sun produces all that is needed materially and the spiritual sun (Son) provides all our inner yearnings.

Their simplistic nature brings all things in easy focus for us to peruse and comprehend.

The Moon reflects generosity and sharing. These qualities will be reflected in you no matter what sign your Moon is in.

Negative Expression: A **55** on the negative path is burdened with karma because they have chosen the wrong path for their expression. There are many paths up the mountain that we can choose from, and each one of us has a particular direction and path to reach the top. Some paths have a lot of rock and shadows to combat, and if we succumb to defeat and start down the mountain again we lose track of our gifts. Every path contains energy, love, ethics, goals and much more that each person's inner self relates to in different degrees. On the lowest vibration, **55**'s are in darkness, cannot find their path and become victims of life.

Dormant Self Number 66

Number **66** is the personification of love. An inner knowingness of the freedom of love pours out this vibration to all around. The inner self knows the perfection of love—that love just IS—that love is not *because*. Number **66**'s love people, animals, plants, sculpture, family, marriage, partners, paintings, books, spiritual values, and just about everything depending where their interests are. They take care of family, plants, marriage, the people in their lives. They don't classify people into good, better or best, they see only the loving side.

They do prefer cleanliness as this is part of loving—they take care of themselves and the things for which they are responsible.

The Moon reflects love. A loving responsibility will be added to the traits symbolized by the sign your Moon is in.

Negative Expression: If **66**'s feel they are not getting enough love in return, they may move down scale and express the negative vibration of this number. They may begin to exhibit selfishness towards those close to them, withholding loving attention until they receive a reward. This would be using love to enslave another—feeling that if they give they must get something back in return. Their inner selves becomes clouded with all those unfinished expressions of love and they despair of ever repairing the relationship. The solution is simple when they remove the barriers by seeing what they actually are— unexpressed love—so they can give some love away by giving service to another. A good boy scout always does one good deed a day—why not try two or three?

Ability Numbers

The following list contains a positive and negative interpretation of the ability numbers. This number relates to the ascendant in your birth chart. Even though your ascendant could be any one of the twelve zodical signs (or types), the ability number vibration will be added to the qualities that are indicated by the sign of your ascendant.

Ability Number 1

You are an independent thinker, and behind your original and creative ideas is the drive to put them into operation quickly and efficiently. As creator and inventor you lead instead of following. You could become the head of any business that requires a person who can think on their feet. You could be a governor, general, chief executive, explorer, a civil engineer, legislator, politician, actor, actress, musician, or involved in any field that needs creative ability be it business or in the arts. In investment circles, you may buy and sell with skill for you project far into the future with your planning. You see opportunities and have the spirit to go into action on your decisions. Seldom do you let the opinions of others sway you from your projected goal.

Since you are a pioneer in many fields, there are few who could advise you anyway.

Your innate independence produces a pioneering direction. Learn to think for yourself; be radiant and individualistic.

Ascendant: Exhibits creative tendencies toward profession. Add to your ascendant sign the ability to be an independent thinker and worker.

Negative Expression: The carrying out of creative ideas requires a great deal of ego. The extreme is arrogance which can alienate you from followers. Try not to become impatient with the slower thinking or acting employees (or co-workers) for this path will lead to frustration and lack of achievement. If too many obstacles get in your way it could produce an overbearing effect toward those around you because your capabilities would be challenged. You are the leader and promoter; don't be dictatorial.

Ability Number 2

You would make a fine diplomat since you are sensitive to the reasoning on both sides of a problem. You can put people at ease so that agreements can be discussed in a calm atmosphere. You are the touchstone people need since your presence in any gathering (business or social) guarantees a smooth conference. The bold leaders (1's) of this world need your finesse to arrange terms between warring factions. You are the mediator in critical situations. Number 2's are statesmen, psychologists, secretaries, comptrollers, psychics, mediums, claim adjusters, carpenters, servants, accountants and fiction writers. You have an innate sense of rhythm which contributes to dance, martial arts, painting, writing, partnership, skill in sports and anything related to flow and form. Your emotional sensitivity is tuned to the metaphysical side of life; you can "tune" into others to assist them and yourself with your clairvoyant potential.

Ascendant: Exhibits diplomatic tendencies toward work or profession. You can be an excellent mediator and add that trait to those symbolized by the sign on your ascendant.

Negative Expression: Your peacemaking abilities may not be understood by other people as they mistake this for either peace at any price or a sign of weakness. This in turn makes you vulnerable to overt natures and loud protestations. You can be hurt by unkind words and deeds as you are extremely sensitive to the vibrations of others. If this hurt develops into frustration, you may want to "even" things out and get back at someone. You could also become sullen and cruel in order to settle differences.

Ability Number 3

You are the entertainer no matter what career you choose. Your ability lies in expression through music—as a composer, playing an instrument, working on stage. The artist in you could also be expressed through writing (probably humorous), drawing, lecturing, painting, jewelry making or designing. You can communicate with people in all walks of life for you are witty and charming, and you can help others become light-hearted. A cheerful atmosphere contributes to your best outgoing nature. This is also the number of strength, a thrust forward that pulls many people into your space and forward with you.

This versatility leads you into many vocations as you have many talents. Your intuitive vibration could assist many people to see the bright and shining part of life.

Ascendant: Expresses the beauty of structure. Versatility is a trait that will be added to those inherent in the sign on your ascendant.

Negative Expression: Hopping from one job to another, if done without forethought, could result in becoming trivial and uneffective. Number 3's may become conceited because they exaggerate their own importance and become the prima donnas who want the center of the stage ALL the time. Jealousy enters on green feet to suppress the understudy or the co-worker as 3's become intolerant.

Ability Number 4

You are the organizer, the one who places articles in their proper place, the one who systematizes an office, a company, a thought, or a viewpoint. You know how to get things together and keep them functioning properly. You are a hard worker, loyal to your employer and employees, a conscientious manager who does not shun detail or routine. You could work in any field which stresses numbers, such as accounting, computer science, as a chemist, electrician, engineer, or a teacher in a related field. Your responsibility to your profession should require economical and sincere dedication in order to fulfull your need for work. Therefore architecture, construction, manufacturing or any profession requiring mechanical ability may interest you. You like to be able to see the results of your work. This is the number of physical manifestation.

Ascendant: In any astrological sign you will exhibit some form of organized structure. Your profession and any new beginning will be colored by the traits of your ascendant's sign plus an ability to create systems.

Negative Expression: Because your nature is practical, you may find life a little boring, so some time and money should be spent in having fun. Work hard, but play hard too! Not everything in life fits into a systematic approach. Take another viewpoint once in a while. The positive side of this number gives you the ability to change the structure in your field. Let this part come through more often and do not get stuck in a mold. Relax a little, get out and jog or enter some absorbing sport that contains a lot of action. Your negative side makes you rigid in your opinions, arguing and shouting louder than anyone else just to make your point. If you don't get your own way, you may try to get even using that fine mind to suppress others.

Ability Number 5

Your greatest talent is your ability to cope with the unexpected. You can adapt to a new situation in minutes. You fear nothing and the word "hazard" is not in your dictionary since you know that you "can do." You are the world's greatest salesperson, moving smoothly and confidently from one point to another, leading your customer by the hand and getting the contract signed. You would make a good promoter for sports, business mergers, you could compile advertising campaigns, be a lobbyist, an actor, a civic leader, statesman, lecturer or editor. Public relations, detective work, the secret service, lawyer or scientific inventor are within your realm. A friendly nature such as yours enables you to cope with several situations at one time, handling several customers at once and keeping them all straight. You could play several games of chess or backgammon at one time, keeping the spectators in stitches with your humor. You would be miserable if you could not meet people, so choose an occupation which could stimulate you and give you contact with many types.

Ascendant: In any astrological sign you will be able to adapt to change. The changeability will relate to the actual sign on your ascendant, but you will be more able to cope than other people with that ascendant sign.

Negative Expression: Changing could make you undependable. Over indulgence in sensual pleasures could bring problems in the future. If you find you are exhibiting an unsympathetic tone toward others, look to see where you are coming from—are you indulging in your own superiority, inconsistent in your work or ideals, or are you hostile toward those who can do as well as you do?

Ability Number 6

You are logical and clear thinking, and have the ability to judge right from wrong. You can regulate chaos to create order and harmony. You have the opportunity to become a banker, nurse, architect, physician, welfare worker, teacher, manufacturer, builder, educator, engraver, a dealer in food or home necessities, professional guardian, hotel manager. You can be trusted with the care of the young and of the aged. You could run a day care center, a hospice for young people, a nursing home or you could teach nutrition in these centers. You would do well in the arts as a dramatic actor or a musician. Your timing and rhythm adapts itself to the performing arts. A home life is essential for your happiness as you need a stable base for the security of your family love. You can move into troubled areas to create harmony. Your clear, logical mind can size up situations and evaluate quickly what must be done to bring order out of chaos. This number gives love unstintingly, making you popular with both adults and children. You distribute fair decisions to all and would make a good judge.

Ascendant: will exhibit harmony in all relationships. A sense of fairness and logic will color the natural traits of your ascendant sign.

Negative Expression: In your concern for justice, you need to be careful that you don't meddle in the affairs of others when you are not asked or wanted. Sometimes this may be difficult as your feeling of always being right could be misconstrued by your family, friends, or business associates to be a massive ego trip. Cynicism and egoism about your ability to judge or evaluate character can turn off your friends—remember that the human race is just that—human. You are the cosmic mother, the nurturer of the young and aged, the doorway to higher mind through harmony.

Ability Number 7

Imagination is your keyword—thinking in the abstract, visualizing the future. You want to create a better world to live in so your goal is to examine the way to accomplish this. You can use this ability in business and in your home life. You can be a lawyer, scientist, psychiatrist, watch maker, legislator, electrical expert, or astronomer. You enjoy the detail connected with these occupations and yet get frustrated when employees or co-workers do not move as fast as you do intellectually. You could write technical articles or philosophical treatises. You could indulge in handicrafts, dancing, painting, or building as long as you have ample time to map out in detail your project. You work best alone and in silence or you create your silence so that your analytical mind can research many fields. You should be a specialist in whatever field you choose. You could study the occult, religion, or any subject which requires a deep thinker. You would make a good counselor as your spirit reaches into unknown areas where truths are revealed.

Ascendant: will exhibit a courageous search for truth. This number gives you an ability to forge ahead, especially if you direct yourself to use the energy of the sign on your ascendant at its highest level.

Negative Expression: It is lonely building your consciousness with the protoplasm of high level abstraction. If you humiliate those who do not breathe your rarefied air, you will not establish the planks on your bridge. Suppressing those beneath (?) you will only bring on your own frustration. Learn to build your own rainbow bridge from the mundane to the esoteric. Learn to communicate with other people so you can understand them at their level. You need patience which will not detract from your ability to understand far beyond the average person. Just remember that we all need a little help from our friends, both here and those above.

Ability Number 8

You are the executive who moves steadily toward achievement. You are most successful when concerned with big business. You have the ability to overcome competition for you admit to no limitations. You have enough power in this ability number to choose your business or profession. You would make a good employer as you have good judgment and are fair in your dealings with others. You can reach great heights as an executive and organizer of corporations, or in government and politics. This is called the prosperity number, your rewards coming in money, power and fame through your own efforts. Esoterically, this is also an opportunity for you to study metaphysical material so that you can open (or re-open) your third eye. Number 8 is primal energy; use it where you will but use it wisely.

Ascendant: You exhibit primal energy as you surge toward your goals. This big business energy can be added to the natural traits indicated by the sign on your ascendant.

Negative Expression: You know how the rules are made and where they should be applied so you are apt to feel superior to the rules and regulations. Wealth and power can lead to greediness, so temper your abilities with understanding of the frailties of others. Use diplomacy (when you can stand still for this) instead of steamroller tactics. Develop tolerance and justice for the weaker and less efficient ones without destroying their identities. Lead by your strength instead of pushing. You could be tempted to make your own rules outside of the conventional standards which could culminate in a local or mammoth dictatorship. Suppressing others will only bring your own downfall.

Ability Number 9

This is the number of the true humanitarian. Your ability to understand human conditions could lead you to a successful career in any of the arts or humanitarian organizations. Public work, feature writing, or the physician's healing hand could attract you. Used with a farseeing eye you could influence mankind toward a kinder approach toward the brotherhood of man. Number 9 is the server of mankind. This is done by going out and demonstrating love for other human beings. Evangelists, missionaries, statesmen, soap box orators, and highly educated priests are among this group. All of them are attempting to sway people toward the goodness of life. You would do well in any of the careers which require the kind, humane approach. Civic work, rehabilitation, a defense attorney, holistic healing, the nutritional expert or dietician, philanthropic writing—all these occupations could bring your civilized efforts to the attention of the world.

Ascendant: will exhibit love for your fellow human. Service will be a quality added to the other traits indicated by the sign on your ascendant.

Negative Expression: Watch your financial and emotional resources and do not let them be completely drained from you. While kindness and inspiration are essential for your kind of life and personality, still there are people who would try to gain from your spontaneous extravagance and display of love and generosity. Don't become so sentimental that you dissipate your potential for good with aimless dreaming.

Ability Number 11

You are highly intuitive and psychic, an inspired thinker who is able to communicate at all levels to all people. And what's more, they understand you because you do not talk "above" them. By tuning into their auras, you can divine where they are—yet you do not preach— you magnetize their thoughts toward you by asking the right questions. Your magnetic personality draws people's inner feelings out into the open where they can deal with the problem. You pose questions leading to the revealing of their secret desires. Your psychic ability could lead you into teaching philosophy, gestalt methods of discovery of humanistic principles, or working with awareness groups that are so popular. You can do two tasks at once, handling more than one career simultaneously, and very well, thank you! You have an affinity for music, filmmaking, dancing, poetry, painting, and all vocations associated with fine arts; you could also become a minister, a religious writer, or become involved with aviation, television or radio.

Ascendant: will exhibit your intuitive approach to all professions. This intuition and psychic ability will be added to the natural traits of your ascendant sign.

Negative Expression: Keep your ideals on the positive plane where you can be an inspiration to the people around you. With your inner priestliness, you could become a martyr to your ideals, especially if you get frustrated or begin to get anxious about your psychic ability. This number is so high on the intuitive plane that if expressed in a repressive manner you could go farther downhill than the average person. Be careful of experiments with drugs, especially hallucinogenics. Fame can be yours if you can get the show on the road! It's hard for 11's to get started on careers or a change in career. A low vibration of this number manifests as dishonesty with yourself and with others.

Ability Number 22

This number is linked with many famous and successful people. Anything you wish to accomplish in a material way is possible for you. No door is closed to you—whether your interest is in politics, communication, law, or commerce. You are the master organizer and doer. You can explore new fields of endeavor and work with others to settle the details necessary in good planning.

If you start at the bottom with a corporation, your talents in handling people will soon be recognized and you will be promoted to the top. You can be a builder of beautiful structures, or become a famous actor or actress, a statesman, a famous comedian, an explorer, or a musician. Whatever your gifts, you can rise to your fullest expression of the master number. Develop your potential to the utmost for you belong to the world and it needs your intelligent approach. Whatever you visualize can be yours to build.

Usually this Master Number carries the mark of excellent health as 22's are too busy looking forward to bother about petty complaints. They can tell their bodies to heal themselves (physically, emotionally and mentally) and they will. You also excel in sports.

Ascendant: exhibits master intelligence. This trait combines with the natural tendencies of your ascendant sign and can be used to help you really get ahead in your profession.

Negative Expression: If you lose sight of your potential energy for great deeds and selfless accomplishments, you could become merely greedy and ruthless. Remind yourself that you are the master planner, that you have power on all planes, that you know the universal direction the masses need to go. Don't waste your time in pettiness and gossip, your mission is too important to indulge in this time–wasting expression of this number. Also, if you are not operating fully on the 22 vibration, you may be working on the 4. This is an excellent number, but you would not be working up to your full potential.

Ability Number 33

You are or can become the emotional master. The emotions go from deepest depression up to receptive, exhilarating channels for incoming cosmic rays of ecstasy. You can learn to experience these emotions and share the knowledge of how to move vertically through hate, anxiety, and anger patterns up to a life worth living more fully—responsive to the higher emotional vibrations of love and caring. We all experience individual as well as group emotions. Every meeting of two or more people generates a type of emotion. You can learn (or may have already learned) how to operate on the upper scale of your emotions so that projects can go forward rather than being tabled month after month. You are the one who can sway a group or a committee one way or another, depending or whether you are working on the positive or negative side of this number. Your charm and ability to spot exactly just where members of a group are coming from puts you in a position of power. Choose an occupation which includes some kind of personnel work: a minister, head of a large corporation, head of a division of a factory, buyer for a store or stores, manager of a company or companies, lecturer, actor, leader of awareness groups, or any occupation that will keep you in touch with people.

Ascendant: In any astrological sign you exhibit mastery of the emotions.

Negative Expression: This is an intense vibration to handle. If **33**'s fall into the trap of trying to suppress emotions, they are putting a loose cap on a volcano. Then pow! They explode in all directions, letting their anger flow out toward anyone, striking out at the wrong target—in general, getting into a lot of trouble. Number **33**'s need to understand the emotions, how they are catalogued, and how emotions can be changed from low to higher vibrations. If **33**'s use this information to control others they will eventually get into trouble.

Ability Number 44

Logic is part of a mental process. Aristotle devised two-valued logic—right and wrong. Then came the three-valued logic which is used by engineers and scientists—right, wrong, and maybe. There is also your side, my side, and the correct side. We can take a quantum jump to infinite-valued logic, meaning that we could be more right at one time than another or vice versa—there is infinite distance on either side of the seesaw of logic. Number **44**'s have the ability to judge where on the scale of logic the situation sits. They approach each inquiry with fact finding clarity. They equate "this" with "that" until a clear logical solution emerges. If you are born with this number, you are the mental master, the universal builder with insight, and you have power on a high level that can institute reform for the good of mankind. On the positive side, it's easy for you to carry through plans because you do your homework in advance, facing opposition with charts or proposals that prove your various points. Choose your occupation so you can exercise your ability—law, medicine, healing, computer science, or scientific research would be excellent.

Ascendant: In any astrological sign exhibits your mastery of mental process.

Negative Expression: Sometimes **44**'s convince themselves that the way to go higher is to ingest something to assist the mind to expand. Some experiments along this line have very interesting results for hallucinogenics open channels to both past lives and negative vibrations. If a person cannot handle these powerful negative vibrations, they literally blow their circuits. Meditation without drugs, or intensive study, can open channels but we can handle the information more easily than when we use drugs to do it. A low level of vibration of this number leads to mental cruelty to others.

Ability Number 55

How wonderful if you have this ability number! In addition to the good things you have already read about **55** you will notice that 55 reduced to **10** brings in higher mind. Then **10** reduced to **1** brings in the creative principle. This combination indicates that you have creative principle operating through higher mind bringing life in abundance. You also have the combination of the **11** and **44** to express in your life—idealism plus mental mastery. A further breakdown will give you **11** plus **22** plus **22** which is idealism expressed in physical mastery doubly blessed. Number **22** and **33** also combine to express physical and emotional mastery. This number represents life force, the energy to move in the light of knowledge from higher beings, the inspired and inspiring person. This number acts as a prism bringing the light and then breaking it down into seven rainbow colors (or rays). These colors and rays are visible to everyone, for we feel and relate to a particular color or ray that the number emits.

Ascendant: In any astrological sign this number exhibits life energy and the creative principle.

Negative Expression: All master numbers have a stepped up vibration that some people are unwilling to handle. We only need to handle that which we understand, however, we can learn to understand this vibration by meditating and contacting our guides, our angels and higher beings as mentioned earlier. The other caution is to not use this energy to take away another's life force by physical means or by mental cruelty. Do not take away another person's motivation, or faith in himself or herself. The karma burdened person cannot emit the light of this number. Ability becomes shadowed by darkness and the **55** becomes a victim of life instead of being victorious.

Ability Number 66

This is the master love energy number. This is your expression of universal love for all mankind. You send out loving rays to those around you from your stable base of knowing that love is really where "it's at." This self-realization enables you to take the risk of stating your views on subjects concerning world situations. You are the one who marches with the spirit of Martin Luther King, Jr. and related personalities who want to see equality brought to all the nations' peoples. As the keeper of the love flame, you need to share your views and teach how to accomplish this circle of love around the world. This is the Yin and the Yang, the female and male energy coming together to make the whole being. Number **66** is truly the cosmic mother; the double **6** leads to the **9**, i.e., $6 \times 6 = 36$ and $3 + 6 = 9$, which is brotherly love. The potential is to leave this earthly plane, when you are ready, and move forward into the next plane to read the scrolls in the House of Scrolls to become a more enlightened spirit. $6 + 6 = 12$ and $1 + 2 = 3$, which is an outgoing personality, the person who expresses beliefs with humor and deep understanding.

Ascendant: In any astrological sign this number exhibits the highest level of love.

Negative Expression: The tendency to enslave another is a very low vibration of this number. Operating on the negative side of **66**, you could insist that your mate do many weird things "in the name of love." A negative **66** could also gather many people into his or her camp by selling them the idea that this "is the only way to redemption" and "follow me to strange countries to make a commune and stay pure in love with these revelations that I have received." If you do this, you bring a lot of karma into your future.

Combination Numbers

The following section has been included to help you understand the combination numbers. In order to thoroughly understand the letters in your name, you can interpret the compound numbers to get an even deeper understanding of how your letters vibrate in the universe. For example, a **2** may be a combination of 11 or 38 or 92. Each of these numbers has its own special meaning. These symbolic numbers lead to advanced interpretation, and it is best to understand the basic numbers before concentrating on these. If you don't understand how to interpret these numbers, go back to Chart 1 on page 22, for Carla's expanded numbers have been interpreted there.

The Combinations for Number 1

As you add the value of the letters in your name, you will arrive at a total (before reduction) of one of the compound numbers below:

19 28 37 46 55 64 73 82 or 91

All the above numbers reduce to 10 and then 1. These compound numbers are analyzed as follows:

19 = 1 + 9: Creativeness expressed through brotherly love.

28 = 2 + 8: Cooperate with self and others to bring power to self. Opening of the third eye.

37 = 3 + 7: Communication is important in order to free the self to become a spiritual healer.

46 = 4 + 6: Heal bodies by bringing down the magnetism from above and passing your hands above the body without touching; be harmonious with self and patient.

55 = 5 + 5: Creative healing can bring life energy to self and others. Use your imagination.

64 = 6 + 4: Harmonize self and others by using your higher levels of consciousness. Meditate.

73 = 7 + 3: The bridge from mundane living to esoteric principles is calling you to cross over and communicate with higher beings.

82 = 8 + 2: A power structure or the opening of the third eye comes through someone's assistance and cooperation.

91 = 9 + 1: Brotherly love and success are expressed through creative work.

10 = 1 + 0: Creative mind working with the All. Number **10** is also the pipeline to higher mind.

The compound numbers lead to the interpretation of the single digit, or Master Number, of each category. Use the combinations on pages 13-17 for in-depth interpretations.

Example: 37 = 3 + 7 = 10 = 1 + 0 = 1. Communication (**3**) is important in order to free (**7**) the self to become a spiritual healer (**7**) by using the pipeline to higher mind (**10**), thereby finding new ways to express creativity (**1**).

The Combinations for Number 2

As you add the value of the letters in your name you will arrive at a total (before reduction) of one of the compound numbers listed below:

$$11\ 20\ 29\ 38\ 47\ 56\ 65\ 74\ 83 \text{ and } 92$$

some reducing to 11 and then to **2**.

$$11 = 1 + 1 = \mathbf{2}$$
$$20 = 2 + 0 = \mathbf{2}$$
$$29 = 2 + 9 = 11 = 1 + 1 = \mathbf{2}$$
$$38 = 3 + 8 = 11 = 1 + 1 = \mathbf{2}$$
$$47 = 4 + 7 = 11 = 1 + 1 = \mathbf{2}$$
$$56 = 5 + 6 = 11 = 1 + 1 = \mathbf{2}$$
$$65 = 6 + 5 = 11 = 1 + 1 = \mathbf{2}$$
$$74 = 7 + 4 = 11 = 1 + 1 = \mathbf{2}$$
$$83 = 8 + 3 = 11 = 1 + 1 = \mathbf{2}$$
$$92 = 9 + 2 = 11 = 1 + 1 = \mathbf{2}$$

These compound numbers are analyzed as follows:

$11 = 1 + 1$: Creativity rising to a rebirth of ideas.

$20 = 2 + 0$: Sensitivity to the All.

$29 = 2 + 9$: The peacemaker uses compassion.

$38 = 3 + 8$: The inspirational person moves with hidden powers.

$47 = 4 + 7$: Patience and analysis bring rewards.

$56 = 5 + 6$: Life abounds through harmony.

$65 = 6 + 5$: Harmony creates new expansive ideas.

$74 = 7 + 4$: The studious and loyal initiate is rewarded.

$83 = 8 + 3$: Leadership and power using good communication.

$92 = 9 + 2$: Universal love brings peace with cooperation.

The compound numbers lead to the interpretation of the single digit, or Master Number, of each category. Use the combinations for in-depth interpretations.

Example: 20 = 2 + 0 = **2**. Sensitivity (**2**) to the All (God, Universal Mind) (**0**) will bring peace (**2**) and ability to counsel (**2**) people intuitively (**2**).

The Combinations for Number 3

As you add the value of the letters in your name you will arrive at a total (before reduction) of one of the compound numbers below:

12 21 30 39 48 57 66 75 84 and 93

some reducing to 12 and then all to **3**.

12 = 1 + 2 = **3**
21 = 2 + 1 = **3**
30 = 3 + 0 = **3**
39 = 3 + 9 = 12 = 1 + 2 = **3**
48 = 4 + 8 = 12 = 1 + 2 = **3**
57 = 5 + 7 = 12 = 1 + 2 = **3**
66 = 6 + 6 = 12 = 1 + 2 = **3**
75 = 7 + 5 = 12 = 1 + 2 = **3**
84 = 8 + 4 = 12 = 1 + 2 = **3**
93 = 9 + 3 = 12 = 1 + 2 = **3**

The above is analyzed as follows:

12 = 1 + 2: The creative principle must work through cooperation and tact.

21 = 2 + 1: Patience is needed to do creative counseling.

30 = 3 + 0: Communication at a very high level.

39 = 3 + 9: An expression of love for mankind.

48 = 4 + 8: Manifesting success and/or opening the third eye.

57 = 5 + 7: Creative healing through spiritual awareness.

66 = 6 + 6: Self-realization. The doorway to the higher mind is through love.

75 = 7 + 5: Healing spiritual gaps with the creative mind.

84 = 8 + 4: The third eye can be opened by studious application of energy received from higher beings.

93 = 9 + 3: Universal love is communicated to others.

The compound numbers lead to the interpretation of the single digit, or Master Number, of each category. Use the combinations for in-depth interpretations.

Example: $39 = 3 + 9 = 12 = 1 + 2 = 3$, an expression (**3**) of love of mankind (**9**) can be brought about by discovering new ideas (**1**), and cooperating with others (**2**) will assist the communication (**3**).

The Combinations for Number 4

As you add the value of the letters in your name you will arrive at a total (before reduction) of one of the compound numbers below:

13 22 31 40 49 58 67 76 85 or 94

some reducing to 13 and all reducing to **4**.

$$13 = 1 + 3 = 4$$
$$22 = 2 + 2 = 4$$
$$31 = 3 + 1 = 4$$
$$40 = 4 + 0 = 4$$
$$49 = 4 + 9 = 13 = 1 + 3 = 4$$
$$58 = 5 + 8 = 13 = 1 + 3 = 4$$
$$67 = 6 + 7 = 13 = 1 + 3 = 4$$
$$76 = 7 + 6 = 13 = 1 + 3 = 4$$
$$85 = 8 + 5 = 13 = 1 + 3 = 4$$
$$94 = 9 + 4 = 13 = 1 + 3 = 4$$

The combinations are analyzed as follows:

13 = 1 + 3: The creative principle working through communication to logical answers (**4**).

22 = 2 + 2: Sensitivity to others bringing peace.

31 = 3 + 1: An intuitive counselor unafraid to move into creative areas.

40 = 4 + 0: The physical healer working through the all to bring health to many.

49 = 4 + 9: The logical mind working through love of mankind.

58 = 5 + 8: Travel in body and/or mind creates power, money, or opening of third eye.

67 = 6 + 7: Harmony is possible by using the logical, orderly mind as a bridge to freedom.

76 = 7 + 6: Wise use of self-realization brings energy and harmony to projects.

85 = 8 + 5: Power and intuition work with logic.

94 = 9 + 4: Universal love can heal the etheric body.

The compound numbers lead to the interpretation of the single digit or Master Number of each category. Use the combinations for in depth interpretations.

Example: 31 = 3 + 1 = **4**, an intuitive counselor (**3**) is unafraid to move into creative (**1**) areas to manifest what is needed (**4**), or perform healing for someone (**4**).

The Combinations for Number 5

As you add the value of the letters in your name you will arrive at a total (before reduction) of one of the compound numbers below:

14 23 32 41 50 59 68 77 86 and 95

some reducing to 14 and than all reducing to **5**.

14 = 1 + 4 = **5**
23 = 2 + 3 = **5**
32 = 3 + 2 = **5**
41 = 4 + 1 = **5**
50 = 5 + 0 = **5**
59 = 5 + 9 = 14 = 1 + 4 = **5**
68 = 6 + 8 = 14 = 1 + 4 = **5**
77 = 7 + 7 = 14 = 1 + 4 = **5**
86 = 8 + 6 = 14 = 1 + 4 = **5**
95 = 9 + 5 = 14 = 1 + 4 = **5**

The above is analyzed as follows:

14 = 1 + 4: Creative principle working with logic.

23 = 2 + 3: Patience is required of the intuitive counselor.

32 = 3 + 2: Better communication is needed to get cooperation.

41 = 4 + 1: Manifest what is needed through leadership.

50 = 5 + 0: Life energy manifesting through the All.

59 = 5 + 9: Life energy expressed through brotherly love.

68 = 6 + 8: Harmony brings the third eye under control.

77 = 7 + 7: Wisdom and faith seek spiritual freedom.

86 = 8 + 6: Opening of the third eye requires harmony in relationships.

95 = 9 + 5: Brotherly love expands by using a variety of experiences that take advantage of every opportunity to grow.

The compound numbers lead to the interpretation of the single digit or Master Number of each category. Use the combinations for in-depth interpretations.

Example: 32 = 3 + 2 = **5**, better communication (**3**) is needed to get cooperation (**2**) in order to venture (**5**) farther afield to get new customers, new ideas or new spiritual growth.

The Combinations for Number 6

You will arrive at a total (before reduction) of one of the compound numbers below:

15 24 33 42 51 60 69 78 87 or 96

and some reducing to 15 and all reducing to **6**.

$$15 = 1 + 5 = \textbf{6}$$
$$24 = 2 + 4 = \textbf{6}$$
$$33 = 3 + 3 = \textbf{6}$$
$$42 = 4 + 2 = \textbf{6}$$
$$51 = 5 + 1 = \textbf{6}$$
$$60 = 6 + 0 = \textbf{6}$$
$$69 = 6 + 9 = 15 = 1 + 5 = \textbf{6}$$
$$78 = 7 + 8 = 15 = 1 + 5 = \textbf{6}$$
$$87 = 8 + 7 = 15 = 1 + 5 = \textbf{6}$$
$$96 = 9 + 6 = 15 = 1 + 5 = \textbf{6}$$

The above is analyzed as follows:

15 = 1 + 5: The creative principle moves in many directions.

24 = 2 + 4: The idealist can manifest physical healing.

33 = 3 + 3: The intuitive counselor can bring in higher knowledge so it can be communicated to others.

42 = 4 + 2: Physical healing occurs when both parties are in agreement.

51 = 5 + 1: Creative mind brings rebirth of ideals.

60 = 6 + 0: The self-realized person is working with the All.

69 = 6 + 9: Self-realization occurs through brotherly love.

78 = 7 + 8: Freedom to move through the eye of the needle awakens the third eye.

87 = 8 + 7: Prosperity comes through analyzing facts.

96 = 9 + 6: Awareness of the love of mankind awakens the nurturing aspect.

The compound numbers lead to the interpretation of the single digit or Master Number of each category. Use the combinations for in-depth interpretations.

Example: 69 = 6 + 9 = 15 = 1 + 5 = **6**, self-realization occurs through brotherly love (**9**) by using creative mind (**1**) to expand (**5**) harmonious (**6**) relationships.

The Combinations for Number 7

As you add the value of the letters in your name you will arrive at a total (before reduction) of one of the compound numbers below:

16 25 34 43 52 61 70 79 88 and 97

some reducing to 16 and all reducing to **7**.

16 = 1 + 6 = **7**
25 = 2 + 5 = **7**
34 = 3 + 4 = **7**
43 = 4 + 3 = **7**
52 = 5 + 2 = **7**
61 = 6 + 1 = **7**
70 = 7 + 0 = **7**
79 = 7 + 9 = 16 = 1 + 6 = **7**
88 = 8 + 8 = 16 = 1 + 6 = **7**
97 = 9 + 7 = 16 = 1 + 6 = **7**

The combinations are analyzed as follows:

16 = 1 + 6: Creative principle moves with harmony.

25 = 2 + 5: The idealist can use creative mind.

34 = 3 + 4: The intuitive counselor can manifest those things he or she desires.

43 = 4 + 3: Manifestation of wants comes from higher beings.

52 = 5 + 2: Creative healing takes place when both parties agree.

61 = 6 + 1: Nurturing love finds new ways to creativity.

70 = 7 + 0: The healer works with the All to fill spiritual gaps.

79 = 7 + 9: The bridge from the mundane to the spiritual occurs only with humanitarian principles.

88 = 8 + 8: Power, fame and glory through total knowing of the spiritual principles.

97 = 9 + 7: Brotherly love completes the bridge from the mundane to the perfected wisdom and faith.

The compound numbers lead to the interpretation of the single digit or Master Number of each category. Use the combinations for in-depth interpretations.

Example: 52 = 5 + 2 = **7**, creative healing takes (**5**) place when both parties agree (**2**) to use their ability to analyze (**7**) their theories and find the hidden truth (**7**).

The Combinations for Number 8

As you add the value of the letters of your name you will arrive at a total (before reduction) of one of the compound numbers below:

17 26 35 44 53 62 71 80 89 or 98

some reducing to 17 and all reducing to **8**.

$$17 = 1 + 7 = \mathbf{8}$$
$$26 = 2 + 6 = \mathbf{8}$$
$$35 = 3 + 5 = \mathbf{8}$$
$$44 = 4 + 4 = \mathbf{8}$$
$$53 = 5 + 3 = \mathbf{8}$$
$$62 = 6 + 2 = \mathbf{8}$$
$$71 = 7 + 1 = \mathbf{8}$$
$$80 = 8 + 0 = \mathbf{8}$$
$$89 = 8 + 9 = 17 = 1 + 7 = \mathbf{8}$$
$$98 = 9 + 8 = 17 = 1 + 7 = \mathbf{8}$$

The above is analyzed as follows:

$17 = 1 + 7$: Creativity helps to bridge unknowingness by analysis.

$26 = 2 + 6$: Regeneration of the body is possible by harmonizing mind and spirit with body.

$35 = 3 + 5$: Acquire knowledge from higher beings by exploring meditative processes.

$44 = 4 + 4$: Mental mastery. Organization and responsibility go hand in hand.

$53 = 5 + 3$: The expansive creative mind requires expression and communication with others.

$62 = 6 + 2$: Energy flows inward for self-realization through patience.

$71 = 7 + 1$: Research with wisdom finds a creative outlet.

$80 = 8 + 0$: The third eye is opening to receive solar energy.

$89 = 8 + 9$: Power and control of self are obtained through humanitarian effort.

$98 = 9 + 8$: Successful ventures require strong foundations.

The compound numbers lead to the interpretation of the single digit or Master Number of each category. Use the combinations for in-depth interpretations.

Example: $89 = 8 + 9 = 17 = 1 + 7 = $ **8**. Power and control of self (**8**) are obtained through humanitarian (**9**) effort using independent (**1**) thought to analyze where he or she is coming from (**7**).

The Combinations for Number 9

As you add the value of the letters in your name you will arrive at a total (before reduction) of one of the compound numbers below:

18 27 36 45 54 63 72 81 90 or 99

some reducing to 18 and all reducing to **9**.

$$18 = 1 + 8 = \mathbf{9}$$
$$27 = 2 + 7 = \mathbf{9}$$
$$36 = 3 + 6 = \mathbf{9}$$
$$45 = 4 + 5 = \mathbf{9}$$
$$54 = 5 + 4 = \mathbf{9}$$
$$63 = 6 + 3 = \mathbf{9}$$
$$72 = 7 + 2 = \mathbf{9}$$
$$81 = 8 + 1 = \mathbf{9}$$
$$90 = 9 + 0 = \mathbf{9}$$
$$99 = 9 + 9 = 18 = 1 + 8 = \mathbf{9}$$

The combinations are analyzed as follows:

$18 = 1 + 8$: The creative principle uses positive leadership to attain success.

$27 = 2 + 7$: Physical healing is possible through research and analysis.

$36 = 3 + 6$: Acquire knowledge from higher beings by harmonizing your physical, emotional and mental bodies.

$45 = 4 + 5$: Etheric body healing is possible through expansion of consciousness.

$54 = 5 + 4$: Abundant life through loyalty.

63 = 6 + 3: Harmonize your intuitive knowledge as you thrust forward in universal love.

72 = 7 + 2: Wisdom is necessary to diplomatically handle universal issues.

81 = 8 + 1: Power and success are possible through creative love.

90 = 9 + 0: Brotherhood for all mankind combines universal love with solar energy.

99 = 9 + 9: Gifts of universal love, compassion and synthesis bring perfection.

The compound numbers lead to the interpretation of the single digit or Master Number of each category. Use the combinations for in-depth interpretations.

Example: 99 = 9 + 9 = 1 + 8 = **9**, gifts of universal love, compassion (**9**) and synthesis (**9**) bring perfection (**9**) through a strong personality (**1**) to bring rich rewards (**8**) to those who complete their cycles (**9**).

The Combinations for Number 11

As you add the value of the letters in your name you will arrive at a total (before reduction) of one of the compound numbers below:

29 38 47 56 65 74 83 or 92

all reducing to **11**.

29 = 2 + 9 = **11**
38 = 3 + 8 = **11**
47 = 4 + 7 = **11**
56 = 5 + 6 = **11**
65 = 6 + 5 = **11**
74 = 7 + 4 = **11**
83 = 8 + 3 = **11**
92 = 9 + 2 = **11**

The combinations are analyzed as follows:

29 = 2 + 9: Cooperation and diplomacy expressed through compassion will heighten intuition.

38 = 3 + 8: The intuitive counselor achieves recognition through
sharing.

47 = 4 + 7: Loyalty is required to cross the bridge to true consciousness uplifting.

56 = 5 + 6: The expansion of the creative mind is assisted by
metaphysical principles.

65 = 6 + 5: The metaphysical mind needs room to expand and
grow toward idealistic situations.

74 = 7 + 4: Wisdom goes hand in hand with practicality.

83 = 8 + 3: Money and power are possible through good communication with higher beings when the goal is inspirational.

92 = 9 + 2: Understanding of metaphysical principles will bring
physical healing.

The compound numbers lead to the interpretation of the master
number.

Example: 38 = 3 + 8 = **11**, the intuitive counselor (**3**) achieves
recognition (**8**) through sharing and revealing (**11**) truths of an artistic
and mystic philosophy (**11**).

The Combinations for Numbers 22, 33, 44, 55, 66

When we come to the above Master Numbers we need to use a
different system for in-depth interpretation.

Example: K A T H E R I N E   M A C E Y

            2 1 2 8 5 9 9 5 5   4 1 3 5 7

reduced to: 46   20

Add: 46 + 20 = **66**

To arrive at an in-depth interpretation for KATHERINE MACEY'S *abilities*, you would turn to the preceding pages and find 46 and 20 in The Combinations. To find 46 you would add 4 + 6 = 10 = 1 + 0 = **1**, so you would refer to page 13 concerning **1** in The Combinations. To find 20 you would add 2 + 0 = **2**, so you would refer to page 13 concerning **2** in The Combinations.

Remember that the combination interpretations lead to the final number, which in this case is **66**, so you would also refer to **66** in the Table of Numbers for Abilities on page 69.

This particular method can be carried further to the interpretations of the vowels (*desire*) and the consonants (*dormant self*) if you want to go in-depth to find some of the hidden talents, motivations, etc. of a person.

Inclusion Table Numbers

The Inclusion Table, shown in Chart 3 on page 88, takes us a step further in defining a name. You will be using the same evaluation system that we discussed on page 20. This time you will be counting the number of 1's in your name, or the number of 2's in your name, etc. Then you record how many of each number you have in your name by placing the correct count in the proper squares or boxes, as we have shown in Chart 3.

Example:

```
M A R Y   L E E   S M I T H   has a total of 12 letters in her name.
4 1 9 7   3 5 5   1 4 9 2 8
```

Mary has two 1's, one 2, one 3, two 4's, two 5's, no 6's, one 7, one 8, and two 9's in her name. There are a total of twelve letters in her name, and when counting the number of letters, make sure that your numerical total matches the number of letters in the name. Place your count opposite the proper number in the Inclusion Table, as we have shown in Chart 2.

Name _Mary Lee Smith_   Birthdate _____

	8	7	10/1	5 5	9	9	DESIRE	27	9
									Vowels
	M	A	R	Y	L	E	E	S M I T H	Name
	4	9		3 5 5	1 4	2 8			Consonants

13/4		3		15/6	DORMANT SELF	31	4
4 1 9 7	3 5 5	1 4 9 2 8					Total
21/3	13/4	24/6			ABILITIES	58/13	4

INCLUSION TABLE

1	2
2	1
3	1
4	2
5	2
6	0
7	1
8	1
9	2

KARMA NUMBERS
6	

INTENSIFICATION NUMBERS

PLANES OF EXPRESSION

	Mental	Physical	Emotional	Intuitional	
					Inspired
					Dual
					Balanced

FIRST VOWEL _____   CORNERSTONE _____   KEY NUMBER _____

We will now use these Inclusion Table numbers to define three more categories of your life—Karma, Intensification, and Subconscious Response number vibrations.

If you look at the Inclusion Table, you will notice that there is an empty row in Chart 3. The row we filled in represents Mary's birth name. If she had changed her name, you would fill in the second row. If someone has changed their name a number of times, you will have to extend the columns to include all the name changes, especially when you are doing a karmic reading.

We do not use the Master Numbers in Karmic or Subconscious Response readings. However, we do use the Master Numbers in the Intensification number interpretations.

Karmic Numbers (Pluto)

Karma is influenced by the planet Pluto in your astrological chart. The missing numbers (not letters) in the Inclusion Table represent experiences that you have avoided in the past, or experiences where you acted in some way to hurt others. This can also mean a time when you detracted from the survival of others because of your physical, mental, or emotional cruelty.

We avoid looking at karma because we fear it. The symbolism of Pluto is complicated yet beautiful. It has the power to regenerate and remold—to transform and resurrect. On the positive side, Pluto symbolizes the restorer of form and the renewer of life. On the negative side, Pluto represents tribulation, struggle, and destruction.

In Mary's name, we had a missing **6**, so we look for **Karma Number 6** on page 90 in order to interpret her karma. Look up the interpretation of your own karmic numbers.

Karma Number 1

In your past experiences you have refused leadership when positive leadership actions would have produced good things for many people. Or in the past you have used your leadership and creativity to misguide people. If you have avoided initiating new ideas because of fear and ridicule take a definite stand to prove your point.

Karma Number 2

Impatience with your close relationships or business associates will cause a misunderstanding. In your past experiences you have been unwilling to pay attention to details. A hostile attitude will keep you from making wise decisions. Be aware of your challenges and move slowly so you can deliberate each aspect of your ideas. Learn to delegate authority instead of trying to do everything yourself.

Karma Number 3

In your past experiences you scattered your energies in so many diverse directions that chaos prevailed. Chaos promotes misunderstanding between the parties involved. Misunderstandings can move from personal problems to severe public actions like riots. Build your confidence by focusing your attention on one idea at a time until you can express your positive thoughts in a concise manner.

Karma Number 4

Lack of concentration in your past experiences has led to a disorganized frame of mind. Or your rigid concept of right and wrong attitudes brought inflexible, unfair laws into existence. Take a careful look at your decisions. Are you focusing on the best viewpoint for the greatest number of people? Or are you determined to have your own way?

Karma Number 5

In your past experiences you have overindulged in drink, food, drugs or any of the false stimulants as you tried to hide your fear of change when the possibility of change could have assisted many people. You cannot survive for long without understanding your environment and the people who are close. Do not alienate the ones who love you by turning off and turning on to some overindulgence when you crave stimuli.

Karma Number 6

In your past experiences you have wanted to be free of duty to your family and friends. Your interference in people's lives when you were not invited to solve their problems has led to your own problem of not feeling wanted and appreciated. Do not run away from love. If you fail the test of loyalty to your loved ones in this lifetime you will be watching the happiness of others instead of your own.

Karma Number 7

In your past experiences your impulsive non-thinking action has led to the disruption of the normal course of your analytical posture. Build confidence in yourself by completing your cycles of action. Study the unknown and develop the knowledge that you once knew and discarded. Your false pride could keep you away from the complete knowingness of the metaphysical side of life.

Karma Number 8

In your past experiences you mishandled financial matters. Your carelessness with money needs to be examined. Are you afraid of losing something so you grab and pay for it right now instead of looking into future possibilities of gain or loss? Step outside yourself and take an objective look at your life without blaming family, friends or the fellow at the next desk. Are you trying to prove that you are better than others?

Karma Number 9

In your past experiences your emotional outbursts caused havoc with family and friends. Jealousy and fear of loss contributed to the need to hold on to your possessions. Start looking at other's viewpoints and have respect for their feelings. Learn the lesson of Universal Love. In the past you have withheld your love, expecting a return for your lofty favors.

Karma Number 0

This does not mean that you came here karma free. Study all the Karmic numbers and the one which triggers your reaction will be the area which is weak. It is possible that you are here on a vacation this lifetime. Then use this time to improve yourself in all the areas.

Intensification Numbers (Venus)

The Intensification Numbers represent the talents that are easy for you. Many people think of this category as a hobby, an indication of the things that we enjoy doing, things that require little effort. These numbers caution that you don't become bored with this talent. You may take it for granted and not use it for what it's worth.

Venus is a major influence when trying to understand the Intensification Numbers. Venus represents your artistic approach to life. You become interested in or attracted to certain expressions of your individuality through this planet. This energy is also expressed in the love you have for work, profession, or things you do in order to amplify your own sense of beauty and rhythm. Venus helps synthesize various energies so that you can bring a cohesive understanding of a particular talent, or bring a particular natural energy to the point of development where it can be used constructively.

The Venus energy can be manifested from both a positive and a negative point of view. When used positively, Venus is gentle, attractive, polite, courteous; when negative, the energy manifests as indifference, indolence, or a lack of caring in regard to perfecting natural talents.

Intensification Numbers are easy to determine. You have already filled in the Inclusion Table section of your numeroscope, and the Intensification Numbers are just the opposite of the karmic numbers. When you would look at the Inclusion Table for missing numbers to determine karma, you would look at the Inclusion Table to see where you have many numbers to determine your Intensification Numbers.

Chart 4 is an example of how to figure your Intensification Numbers. In this chart, we have used the name John Howard Ruhys. He has a total of 15 letters in his name. When counting up the numbers, we find that John has three 1's, no 2's, one 3, one 4, two 5's, two 6's, one 7, three 8's, and two 9's in his name. His Intensification Numbers would be **1** and **8**, for he has more **1**'s and **8**'s than he does other numbers. In order to interpret this energy, you would look up the meanings for number **1** and **8** on the following table. John shows much courage and energy, and he has original ideas that he is

Name ___ John Howard Ruhys ___   Birthdate ___

DESIRE **23** **5** Vowels

	6			6	1		3	7		Vowels
J	O	H	N	H	O	W	A	R	D	R	U	H	Y	S	Name
1	8	5		8		5	9	4		2	9	8	1	Consonants

DORMANT SELF **58/13** **4**

| 1 | 6 | 8 | 5 | | 8 | 6 | 5 | 1 | 9 | 4 | | 9 | 3 | 8 | 7 | 1 | Total |

ABILITIES **81** **9**

INCLUSION TABLE

1	3
2	0
3	1
4	1
5	2
6	2
7	1
8	3
9	2

KARMA NUMBERS
2	

INTENSIFICATION NUMBERS
1
8

PLANES OF EXPRESSION

	Mental	Physical	Emotional	Intuitional
Inspired				
Dual				
Balanced				

FIRST VOWEL **O = 6** CORNERSTONE **J = 1** KEY NUMBER **2**

Chart 4. John Howard Ruhys

willing to promote (see **1**). The combination of the **8**'s and the **1**'s give him the ability to put all this energy and talent to work in order to attain his goals.

Look for the interpretation for your own Intensification Numbers on the following pages. Remember that these numbers represent the talents and abilities you have brought with you from other lifetimes.

If you have any Master Numbers in your name, mark them down separately after you subtract them from their single digits. You may find that the Master Number interpretations in this list are very helpful to you.

Intensification Number 1

Many **1**'s show strong opinions and original ideas which are sometimes promoted through sheer dominance over others. They show much courage and vital energy. Action hobbies, active sports and active participation in some kind of work is necessary in order to focus this vital energy of Venus.

Intensification Number 2

Many **2**'s show patience with others in hobbies that require detail, grace and rhythm. This sensitivity could make a good chess player. These people adapt themselves to others' interests instead of promoting their own.

Intensification Number 3

Many **3**'s show the gift of imagination and expression in words. Any hobby which requires a great deal of communication and fun interests **3**'s. They are light hearted, social, and good mixers.

Intensification Number 4

Many **4**'s show a sense of values, a love of form and work. They find it easy to discipline themselves and sometimes put forth a lot of effort into their hobbies. Any hobby that requires diligent application would interest a **4**.

Intensification Number 5

Many 5's show a love of change, an opportunity for publicity, haste, impulsiveness and pleasure. They adapt easily as long as their hobbies are challenging and active.

Intensification Number 6

Many 6's show a willingness to assume responsibility and effect harmony with the other participants. More than two 6's show cosmic responsibilities. Handicrafts, dancing and volunteer child care (yes 6's would consider this play) would interest them.

Intensification Number 7

Many 7's show a love of facts and mental keenness. They enjoy reading reference catalogues and "how to" books. Mental games and precision sports such as bowling would interest them.

Intensification Number 8

Many 8's have the ability to develop a hobby so they can make money or display expertise in their reach for personal glory—such as sports car racing. They love to collect trophies. They see themselves as winners.

Intensification Number 9

Many 9's show generosity and emotion for the other person when they are playing a sport. Sometimes 9's will even let the other person win in order to save the feelings of the other person or their opponent.

Intensification Number 11

Many 11's show an intuitive seeking for perfection in business and personal pursuits. Hobbies could include rhythmic movement whether in handicrafts, music, or dance.

Intensification Number 22

Many 22's show a love of practical games and active, very competitive sports. They are the scorekeepers.

Intensification Number 33

A **33** in your name would show a highly emotional attitude regarding a hobby. The intense interest in something that is exciting and gives emotional rewards.

Intensification Number 44

A number **44** in your name would show a practical approach to any hobby where you could take the leadership and command.

Intensification Number 55

A **55** in your name would show a vital flow of life force directed toward any hobby. You would inject any game with energy and humor.

Intensification Number 66

This number represents a love energy (tennis anyone?) that encompasses all the players in a field of good communication.

Subconscious Response Numbers (Phaeton)

This category expresses an emotional vibration and shows your response in a crisis situation. The category doesn't express ability, nor does it relate to your conscious action. The Subconscious Response number reflects your positive reaction in a stress situation. When we are under stress, we are capable of tremendous feats of strength, both on physical and mental levels. When this happens, all your experiences in crisis situations—when you have survived by doing something quickly—come up to now, the present time. All your attention is also brought to "now." People lift cars off people and exhibit courage in extreme danger because their intention and their total attention helps them make the correct decision for the moment. All their reserves are there to use, now.

The Subconscious Response numbers are expressing the vibrations of the planet Phaeton, the planet which blew up eons ago and formed the asteroid belt. The energy that was Phaeton's comes together for us in a moment of crisis to assist us to save ourselves and others from danger.

The thing to remember about this category is how you keep your act together. How does the energy of Phaeton affect your actions? Can you bring all the pieces of the jigsaw puzzle (Phaeton) together in order to make a wise decision that will contribute to your and another's survival?

In order to determine your Subconscious Response number, you must subtract the amount of Karma Numbers you have from the number 9. This means you must have a single digit to work with. To illustrate this, please look at Chart 4 on page 93. It is the chart for John Howard Ruhys. His name contains one Karmic Number. If you look at his Inclusion Table, you will see that he had no 2's. We subtract this one Karmic Number from 9 (9 - 1 = 8) and determine that his Subconscious Response number is 8. If someone had more than one Karmic Number (for example, if someone had 3 Karmic Numbers) you would subtract 3 from 9, and the Subconscious Response number would be 6. There are no Master Numbers in this category.

The list of Subconscious Response numbers follows. You may wish to look up your own at this time. We have not included numbers 1 and 2 because no one can have so many karmic numbers in their numeroscope that they would get either 1 or 2 as a Subconscious Response number.

Subconscious Response Number 3

This implies six karmic lessons. It is rare that anyone would exhibit more karma than this. This number indicates an uncertainty about responses. Vague and scattered reactions would be evident, and if this energy is suppressed from taking action, this person might explode in anger when confronted by a survival issue.

Subconscious Response Number 4

Implies five karmic lessons. This person would react in an overly cautious manner and in such great detail that decisive action is delayed. This person would concentrate on lack of help rather than assisting.

Subconscious Response Number 5

Implies four karmic lessons. This person would be restless, nervous, and dissatisfied with what is happening. He or she would run around in circles instead of creating order out of chaos. Needs to concentrate on one idea or particle at a time.

Subconscious Response Number 6

Implies three karmic lessons. Emanates concern and love for welfare of all in vicinity. Extremely responsible to others. In moments of stress this person's family takes precedence.

Subconscious Response Number 7

Implies two karmic lessons. Analytical approach in all moments of stress. This person will quickly decide how to get the car off a person and will direct others in the execution. He or she is unobstrusive and sensitive to physical and emotional upsets, yet does not appear so on the surface when under strain. This person gets the job done quickly.

Subconscious Response Number 8

Implies one karmic lesson. Can handle unexpected situations efficiently, referring all things to reason. These people may also be figuring how to make a little money out of this stress. On a higher level they have tremendous power, take charge and order people around when physical danger threatens. They make good generals.

Subconscious Response Number 9

Implies no karmic lesson. Crisis situations do not phase this person. He or she can help others and show no compassion. Is impersonal in action, taking care of everyone regardless of personal attachments.

Key Number

You can also add all the numerical values of the first name and reduce them to a single digit or Master Number. This is the second vibration that contacts the newborn child. It is a key that unlocks each experience as it is met. No one key can unlock all the doors, but you can choose to use this key when you wish.

You can compare this number with the Abilities Number (discussed on pages 57–70) and notice the compatibility between the two. If the numbers are the same, this will increase your abilities.

To cite an example, let's look at John Ruhys' Numeroscope again. (See Chart 4 on page 93.) His Key Number is 2. When you look up this 2 under the Basic Numbers (see page 13) you can then compare this number to the 9 that relates to his Abilities. Abilities Number 9 is discussed on page 64. When you compare the two numbers, you may discover that he has to work with the following energy:

His ability to understand people and conditions (9) will assist those with problems if he uses patience (2).

He can bring a peaceful (2) solution to personal and business problems by using his understanding of people. He needs to be aware of the humane approach (9) when he uses his skill (2) and patience (2) to solve problems.

Impatience (negative 2) will create an inconsiderate (negative 9) or selfish (negative 9) act on John's part.

10

How to Interpret Individual Letters

This section will show you how you can better understand people by interpreting the letters in a name. Each separate letter has a vibration of its own. We will discuss the individual interpretations of each letter in the alphabet, how to determine your cornerstone, and how to interpret the first vowel in your name. It is interesting to note how much you can tell about a person when you synthesize the information gleaned from the letters and the numbers in the name.

A.
Creative, original, goes straight to the target, leadership, guided by inspiration.

B.
Shy and needs to be cared for, very sensitive and emotional, withdraws, doesn't take sides.

C.
Psychic, sharing and generous, flowing toward people freely, the symbol for the crescent Moon, symbol for the Trinity.

D.
Practical, reserved, has the ability to handle material matters, self-contained and efficient, reason rules.

E.
Receives from above and below, a helper, talented, capable of great expression and inspiration.

F.
Bears the burdens, hard to make up the mind as intuition tells them to go one way or another, suffers from uncertainty, the cross, very intuitional.

G.
Needs understanding of values, analytical, the most mental of the mental letters, stern, self-controlled but giving.

H.
The ladder from one level to another, refers all things to intelligence, indecisive in actions, wants to advance but vacillates.

I.
The torch—used to light, illuminate or to destroy by fire of the emotions, straight, clear but sometimes deadly, guides up or down, receives from above and below.

J.
Individuality like A but cannot always complete its projects, indecision weakens the ability to lead, could be original and a leader.

K.
Pure inspired intuition, wants to live in an imaginary world; intuitive revelations can manifest as psychic ability, sees the third dimension as a dream—the fifth as a reality.

L.
Generous in a thoughtful manner, cautious, slow and sure without spontaneity, reserved, carefully reasons and then gives opinions.

M.
Well organized though has little vision, least expressive of all the letters, holds things, the valley between the highest expressions, inarticulate.

N.
Imaginative, sees both sides clearly through mental ability, understands intellectually, refers all matters to the mind, wavers if emotionally disturbed so cannot see clearly.

O.
Beautiful, inspired, total, concerned with their own powers which does shut out other opinions, draws life to itself, poised, secure.

P.
Self-sufficient, the quality of **7** may bring on a dichotomy of talk without facts, faith without conviction, seeks facts, quiet and wishes to complete the mental processes before revealing itself.

Q.
Genius level, living in two worlds, physical and intuitional, can receive great quantities of white light which it can use constructively or destructively, tremendous power.

R.
Selfless, understanding, accepting, tolerant, can be imposed upon, strength and power to use for others, handle through the **9**.

S.
Emotional upheaval during this transit, mind is incapable of clear thought because feelings are involved, relates to self more than to others.

T.
Tense, eager for enlightenment, self-sacrificing, constantly strains emotional and physical self, nervously energetic.

U.
Soft, introverted and receptive, able to magnetize the unusual to themselves in an intuitive way, adds strength to any weakness, can attract loss.

V.
Open and receptive to higher planes of consciousness, powerful on the material plane, ability to cut through to the heart of the matter using upper realm guidance.

W.

Self-determinism will enable this person to reach the heights, high goals, limited by depths of emotion, limited by indecision.

X.

Can be high-minded—seeing both sides of the question, this is the challenge to higher learning and self-sacrifice, emotionally strong if it has learned past experience survival techniques.

Y.

Strong intuition which can see through problems and events; a seeker, receiving from above by two channels, goes directly to the solution on the material plane if positive, gifted with higher perception, the double path reaching for information that can be shared materially.

Z.

Like lightning Z has the power to unite heaven and earth, blasting with intuition through the emotions, understands human emotions, unites from the heart to the spirit, healing emotional crises.

Cornerstones

The first letter of your name is your *cornerstone*. It is the first vibratory influence that contacts the newborn child. This letter has a vital hookup with the birth date and should be considered together as influencing the child before and after birth.

This letter gives people the qualities that will assist them in expanding their vibrations—or limiting them—according to the level of their personal expression to the world. This influence is felt on the physical and material plane rather than the spiritual plane.

In Chart 4 on page 93, you will see that John Ruhys has J for the first letter of his name.

The First Vowel

The first spiritual contact that you have with life is indicated by the first vowel in your name. The vowels fall into three categories: positive, receptive, and dual. These categories are not to be confused with the levels of numbers shown in Table 3 on page 12. Positive and receptive vowels are found by *sound*, the dual vowels, by *spelling*, since sometimes a vowel requires two sounds. The positive vowel is long-sounding ("a" as in James), while a receptive vowel is short-sounding ("a" as in Pam). See Table 5 for correct vowel categories.

The first vowel should be placed on your numeroscope chart, the same way that the cornerstone (or first letter of the name) is placed on the chart. In Chart 4 (on page 93) you will see that John's first vowel is "o" and it has been entered in the category marked "first vowel."

After you study your first letter and first vowel, you may wish to refer to the levels of numbers discussed in Table 3 on page 12. Each letter has a general number vibration, and it expresses on three levels. When you understand the cornerstone and the vowel in your name, you can gain even more insight into how this energy is operating within you. And if you don't like what's there, you can change it by becoming conscious of what you are doing.

Table 5. Vowel Pronunciations

Positive	Receptive	Dual
Long A as in James	Short A as in Pam	AI as in Kai
	Short A as in Padre	
Long E as in Lee	Short E as in Beth	EW as in Lewis
Long I as in Mike	Short I as in Dick	AI as in Daisy
Long O as in Joan	Short O as in John	IO as in Violet
Long U as in June	Short U as in Buck	AU as in Laura
Long Y as in Sky	Short Y as in Lynn	

Positive A: Creative, original, authoritative, ambitious, full of fire, open to new ideas, enthusiatic. Firmly grounded to earth, strong will, powerful. Can be intolerant, opinionated, cynical and critical.

Receptive A: Poised and idealistic, the dreamer, sometimes scatters forces and becomes less active, sensitive, retiring. Accepts new ideas readily but may become frustrated when they cannot be put into action.

Dual A: There is some influence of the long A when the sound is the same. The AU sound can indicate a vacillation between ideas. This becomes valuable when both sides of an idea need to be explored; it becomes very negative when used to gossip or carry tales from one to another.

Positive E: Versatile, practical, full of progressive ideas, energetic and resourceful. Illuminates. Searches for the new and unusual and may be too ready to change one good idea for another. Sometimes gets too involved. May find yourself doing six jobs.

Receptive E: Studious and poised, or restless and nervous. Persistent without being aggressive. Determined and reaches goals with confidence. When things get in your way, you tend to lose your composure.

Dual E: Super-sensitive. Reflects other people and their ideas. This sensitivity can be very useful in healing work providing you stay with the patient long enough to accomplish the required result.

Positive I: Direct, they receive from above and below with emotional understanding. The "I" stands for intensity whether working from a positive or negative point. If developed on a higher plane, it is very loving; on an undeveloped plane I's can be cruel and self-indulging.

Receptive I: Quiet, helpful, interested if logic and judgment are present which agree with its emotional reaction. Emotionally withdraws if not in agreement.

Dual I: Needs to strengthen the positive side in order to express itself. Both sides seek expression so there is a little war going on inside because I is very sensitive.

Positive O: Gifted artistically and musically; emotionally inspired, which brings illumination to self and others if working on the positive rather than the negative side of self. Guard against feeling arrogant. Can become arbitrary and domineering since others do not have your mental ability and quickness.

Receptive O: You endure and are the recipient of much protection. This is a happy and social letter, empathizing with others. Can create harmony or disharmony so learn your lessons. You may be reluctant to ask questions.

Dual O: Tolerance, understanding of others and of human nature. Gets involved, need to center yourself so you can know the source of your actions. Needs to learn to act and think that something can be accomplished instead of going around in circles.

Positive U: The gift of writing ability; write from your heart and intuition. Love of beauty and light, likes to be with people. Clairvoyant possibilities. Teacher. Accumulates impractical things.

Receptive U: Selfless, sharing, shy. Tends to be too conservative and secretive. Has great power to give others through intuitive gifts. Can become narrow-minded and miserly.

Dual U: Shift from being carefree to keeping your nose to the grindstone. Aloof from the crowd, easy manner, doing your own thing so it makes you hard to understand—you may seem indifferent.

W: Is sometimes considered a vowel when it follows another vowel. The first vowel would take precedence. It receives from above with double intensity and is capable of higher spirituality. It is free to go where it will. If undeveloped it can become egotistical, conceited and self-indulgent.

Positive Y: The bridge between two worlds and the discoverer of secret doctrines. Being an intuitional dual letter it can take with the left or right hand path. It can reach for guidance and get it, then not know how to use it. May balk and become rigid.

Receptive Y: Must be faced with logic and patience. Does not accept force; don't *tell* them—*show* them—if a person has a Y in his/her name. Secretive, introverts others' opinions on itself.

Dual Y: A stronger first vowel will take precedence.

Note: The **Y** has a two-sided nature, usually described as right and wrong. Intuition is strongest with beliefs deeply ingrained after these beliefs have been carefully examined. **Y** searches for the truth then hesitates about accepting it because of its cautious nature. Does not scatter knowledge but is willing to share it. **Y** brings wisdom down from above from dual sources to reach this third dimensional level where those who listen will benefit.

Dipthongs:

Two vowels together. The first vowel carries the strongest vibration and can be interpreted as shown below:

AA: Leadership, originality, a promoter.

AE: Ambition, talent, energy, understanding, power.

AI: Ambition, inspiration, illumination, has great plans.

AO: Inspired leadership, poised and direct.

AU: Aspiration with intuition, mentally creative.

AW: Contained leadership, hidden values need exposure.

EA: Ambition, energy, power, success, a large ego.

EE: Enthusiasm, physical desires, double talent, understanding.

EI: Mental-emotional energies combine for inspiration.

EO: Freedom, spirituality, harmony, centered in self.

EU: Variety in love relationships, receptive, out-giving.

EW: Energy, power, a researcher, physical endeavors.

IA: The torch bringing clear light into the window of the soul.

IE: Lightning changes through inspiration.

II: Self-centered, in control of self, bringing intuitive knowledge from above and below.

IO: Compassionate, artistic, overly sensitive.

IU: Light expressed in love, the heart side of a person.

IW: Struggles with self in order to reach the highest pinnacle.

OA: Concerned with own powers to lead and inspire others.

OE: Beautifully inspired with own talent, protected.

OI: Artistic with color or music, emotional.

OO: Wants steadfast love, conservative, self-contained, finds it hard to give of self.

OU: Loves beauty, musical, receptive, intuitional.

OW: Searching for other dimensions of endeavor, other worlds.

UA: Active intuition leading in strange directions toward productive projects. Emotional.

UE: Inspired with talent, attracted to fine arts, power gathered and then expressed in truth.

UI: Intuitive power coming from above, feelings can run away with intuition. Needs grounding.

UO: The intuitive well of beauty in expression.

UU: Psychically inclined to gather all knowledge.

UW: Intuition bound by physical senses, needs to understand self in order to progress. A rare combination.

Triple vowels: as in Louise or Louis—need careful scrutiny to find the strongest influence on the positive side.

11

Planes of Expression

Another way that self-expression can be determined is by using the four planes—physical, emotional, mental and intuitional. The letters of the alphabet that relate to the different planes are shown in Table 6 on page 112. If we know the plane in which we have gained the most proficiency—because of our past life experiences and knowledge—we can better promote and direct our activities to succeed in this life. The planes are defined as follows:

Mental Plane: If you have more letters in this column than in the other columns, you have a scientific mind. You have leadership ability and authority. You have the power to explore new ideas in relation to reform, invention, or areas which pertain to using logic and fact. Goals are purposeful and well planned. You could write about serious or technical subjects.

Physical Plane: More letters in this column indicate an interest in human progress in a material way. You could use your energies for tangible results, for you are thoroughly practical. Your type is interested in form and construction. You are usually engaged in work that

Table 6. Planes of Expression

Mental	Physical	Emotional	Intuitional	Total
A	E	I O R Z	K	Inspired
H J N P	W	B S T X	F Q U Y	Dual
G L	D M		C V	Balanced
Total	Total	Total	Total	

requires both physical and mental concentration, so you make an excellent athlete.

Emotional Plane: More letters in this column indicate attributes of an artistic nature. You have a great deal of feeling and appreciation for beauty and nature and a willingness to serve others. Your concern is based on the way your heart moves you, rather than on your reason. Musicians, poets, designers, singers, dancers, architects, photographers and philosophers fit well here. Your emotions are sometimes uncontrolled.

Intuitional Plane: Letters in this column indicate faith and belief in ideas and ideals. You prefer to have things revealed through your intuitional processes than reasoning them through, or by experiencing them through your emotions. You can develop your inner spiritual realm, but the caution is to not lose sight of reality. Your actions are motivated by inspiration. Since there are fewer of these letters in general use, any letters in this column indicate intuitional ability. Several letters in this column indicate psychic ability.

• • •

As you can see from looking at Table 6, there are three categories for each of the four planes. As you consider the various letters of the alphabet and how they relate to your name, you can also see if you function at the inspired level, a balanced level or a dual level combining both. The definition of these categories is as follows:

Inspired: More letters in this section mean you are inspired to start things. You begin actions necessary to reach goals in your life. Fewer letters in this line mean that you are reluctant to start things or embark on new adventures. You are cautious.

Dual: More letters in this column mean you are able to change your direction when necessary. An overbalance of letters in this section (more than on the Inspired or Balanced lines) indicates an inability to make up your mind. You are able to change the form when necessary if balanced by the other two lines. You can take an original idea proposed by someone else and change it into something else or something better. Few letters in this column indicate a rigidity to new ideas.

Balanced: More letters in this section means you are able to stop things. You finish projects. You love to take ideas which have been created by the inspired person, changed by the dual person, and get the job done. You dislike having unfinished cycles in your life. Fewer letters in the section indicates that you have a problem making up your mind and cannot get your pet projects finished.

• • •

In order to calculate this section, you need to enter in all the letters in their proper categories (according to Table 6). All the A's in your entire name go into the Mental–Inspired column. Use the letters—not their numerical values. If you have two R's in your name, be sure to write RR in the Emotional–Inspired column, etc. To make sure that you understand this, let's look at Chart 5 on page 114. Here we are using John Ruhys' chart again. Following the rules set out in Table 6, he has one A, three H's, one J, and one N in the Mental column. These letters are divided between the Inspired, Dual and Balanced columns as well, and you will see that he has no letters in the section for Mental–Balanced. The total for the Mental Plane column, reading from top to bottom, is 6. The total for Mental, Physical, Emotional, and Intuitional columns that make up the Inspired section is 5.

It is important to remember that in this section we are not looking at the amount of letters, but the ratio of the amounts. Most people start more than they can finish. If you find you are over-balanced in any category in Table 6, take a look at where you are coming from. Are

Name _John Howard Rubys_   Birthdate _____

DESIRE

																Vowels
J	O	H	N		H	O	W	A	R	D		R	U	H	Y	S	Name
																Consonants

DORMANT SELF _____ Total

ABILITIES _____

INCLUSION TABLE

1			
2			
3			
4			
5			
6			
7			
8			
9			

KARMA NUMBERS

INTENSIFICATION NUMBERS

PLANES OF EXPRESSION

	Mental	Physical	Emotional	Intuitional		
	A	1	OORR	1	5	Inspired
	HHAJN	W	S	UY	9	Dual
	1	D	1	1	1	Balanced
	6	2	6	2		

FIRST VOWEL _O_   CORNERSTONE _J_   KEY NUMBER _2_

Chart 5. John Howard Rubys

you rigid in your attitudes? Do you finish your cycles? Are you a compulsive finisher—just have to do it right now? All these questions are vital to your expression of your attitude.

When you interpret the columns you are looking at the ratio again. Are the sums of the columns fairly even (except for the intuition column)? Do you lack letters in your physical column? Do you have an over-abundance of letters in your emotional column? Look carefully at the planes: are you more physical in your expression than mental? Are you easily upset (more emotional letters)? Are you truly psychic and do you refuse to recognize this gift? Do you have more than one letter in the intuitional plane?

12

Triadic Communication

Scientists have discovered that our bodies, being electric, radiate energy. Energy flows both ways. Energy flows out to others from us and we accept (or reject) energy that flows toward us. The energy that flows from us contains all our accumulated experiences from our past lives. This outflow contains our emotions and attitudes and sometimes negative vibrations which make up the person we are today. The energy that flows toward us contains all the experiences, emotions, attitudes, etc. of others. We are free to accept or reject these flows, just as others are free to accept or reject what we send out to them.

    To understand these energies better, we can use the vibrations of the letters and numbers in our names to interpret where we are today and how we can benefit ourselves. By understanding these vibrations we can elevate ourselves and move forward into a more productive and spiritual life.

    The triadic communcation pyramid formula was given to me in a meditation. By using this method, you are interpreting the numbers in your name on a higher and deeper level. Please refer to figure 2 on page 118 as we lead you through the explanation of the pyramid.

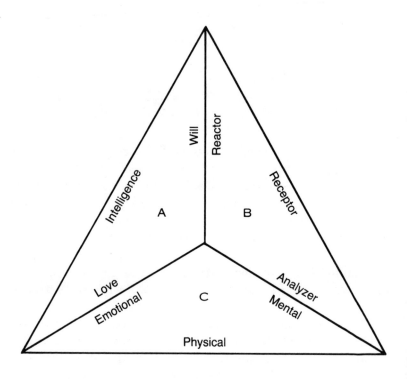

Figure 2. The Triadic Pyramid consists of three parts: A) the Soul Triangle, B) the Mind Triangle, and C) the Body Triangle.

There are three separate triangles in the pyramid; each triangle represents one of your basic selves—the soul, the mind and the body. Each separate triangle represents a composite of three basic energies. We have a total of nine energy flows to discover and understand. You can become aware of these energy flows by using the numerical vibrations of your name.

You come into this lifetime with your soul triangle, you have a mind triangle to develop, and a body triangle in which to live. When the body is okay and the mind is clear and free of trauma, the soul can be reached with ease. Channels are open and glimpses of reality and truth can be fused to your being.

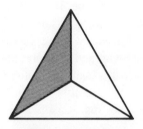

Soul Triangle

The being (you) does not have a soul! The being (you) *is* a *soul*! Which has never been separated from your individual, personalized interpretation of the divine source. You are an individualized soul operating with free choice. Some definitions for soul are: that which is you; the "I"; the "I AM" principle; the Spirit; the higher self; the Prime Mover.

The soul triangle is represented by the first name—the name given to you so you experience certain lessons and vibration for this lifetime. The soul triangle is divided into three energy flows as follows:

The Will of the Father

The Love of the Son

The Intelligence of the Comforter

Will of the Father

The first energy—the Will of the Father—actually indicates the way you receive and express divine will as it comes through you. You find the single digit (or Master Number) by adding the **vowels** of your first name. Use this number to consult the following pages to find the interpretations for your first name **Will Number**, which is influenced by the planet Mars. This number will make you aware of how you have chosen to motivate yourself to express Divine Will, and may help you better define what you should be doing in life.

Will Number 1

The self-determinism to carry out the Father's Will is expressed in new ideas, inventions and progress in many fields for mankind. Number **1** is a little headstrong, wanting people to believe as he or she does, or follow the pathway and take no other than he or she does. These people need to use this leadership *after* listening to their higher selves for then they can use this spiritual knowledge with full knowingness that there are many pathways.

The Mars influence drives **1**'s forward in spite of many obstacles.

Will Number 2

The gentleness apparent in **2**'s can turn many people toward the light. These people cooperate wholly with the Father's Will and are happy in doing so. They wish to serve, and have come here to make peace between brothers, families, and even nations. Their kindness and compassion attract many to their side. Care needs to be taken by **2**'s that they are not lead in a direction contrary to their motivation toward higher spiritual endeavors.

The Mars influence is a warm glow that attracts those who seek salvation and understanding of universal laws.

Will Number 3

The bubbly enthusiasm of **3**'s plus their willingness to embrace the Father's WILL—will influence others. They sincerely want to find a line of communication for spiritual growth. They are the demonstrators and the lecturers. Their sharing is great as long as patience doesn't wear thin at the slower moving people.

The Mars influence rises like the sun to shed light on dark places showing others the light of understanding and loving communications.

Will Number 4

Steadfastly do the **4**'s continue in their Father's Will, working in the vineyard, trimming their lamps and always ready to attend the bridegroom. Their willingness to look at others' viewpoint could limit their spirituality if they are working on the negative side of this number.

The Mars influence is a steady flame. Others can depend on the knowledge that **4**'s will **be there**.

Will Number 5

The radiance of the Father's Will shines through you. You know about the life giving principle that the Father's love brings. Your seeking for personal freedom brings you in contact with many, so watch your impulsive, short-sighted motivations that could abuse your freedom.

The Mars influence radiates to those around you as you bring positive changes to people who are afraid to venture into the very essence of life.

Will Number 6

The Father's Will is demonstrated through you with service to mankind. You are a Cosmic Mother—a nurturer, one who brings harmony as you assist others to deeper understanding of the Universal Laws. Your motivation to take care of the world's problems can be blocked if your emotions get in the way.

The Mars influence is courage that is backed by loving rays that surround and ease the hurts of others.

Will Number 7

The Father's Will cuts through the cloudiness of indecision to bring a pin-point of light to you and to others. This light is sharp and definitive of the truths of the Universe. You may be fearful of showing emotions or admitting to private motivations.

The Mars influence works like a laser beam that cuts through the dross but it may be overlooked.

Will Number 8

The Father's Will is the blue flame that cuts away unessentials, bringing forth the pure light of performance. Your soul motivation is to bring the very best to others and to magnetize the very best out of others. Your motivation is to show others how to prosper spiritually.

The Mars influence is a direct blue flame that hovers above the material candle of physical life—the impetus that provides the heat of accomplishment.

Will Number 9

The Father's Will assists 9's to hold their brothers safe in merciful arms. Your soul desire is to save everyone from evil influences. You are a romantic idealist, out-flowing your love in your desire to protect others. This protective motivation could be misunderstood, so you need to be careful to balance your energies.

The Mars influence is compassion, like the rosy light of dawn breaking over the sea.

Will Number 11

The Father's Will projects through 11, stimulating your incentives to study and discover the secrets of the universe. Your soul desire is to inspire others and then reveal the secrets found through your (11) clairvoyant capabilities.

The Mars influence flashes from the planet to you, inspiring bursts of zealous endeavor.

Will Number 22

The Father's Will is like a contained fire that can be fanned to brilliance by masterly planning. It can then reflect the plans of the ruler of our universe. With this awesome ability comes responsibility for your actions. You can build and you can destroy—choose.

The Mars influence is like a brush fire—igniting the energies of those with whom you come in contact. Control the fire and you can help build a perfect world.

Will Number 33

Our Father has given us free choice so He knows the games we are playing. This emotional number can master the games and work through the human emotions, bringing a higher sensitivity to others. This requires discipline at the soul level, or the willingness to set aside your own reactions to things that upset you in order to clarify the game of life for others.

The Mars influence glitters like tiny solar cells, bringing sensitivity to receptive persons.

Will Number 44

The channels for receiving this high powered energy are open or ready to be opened in this lifetime. The mastery over physical form can be channeled into practical efforts, building edifices to glorify God. You are also motivated to build lofty ideas through your mental prowess.

The Mars influence is similar to the contained power characteristic of the crystal.

Will Number 55

The soul's desire of **55** is to bring life to all living creatures; the song of the clear red-violet flame, breathing the breath of life into the lifeless and discouraged humanity. You quicken the spirit in those who are without hope.

The Mars influence bubbles with newly created life.

Will Number 66

The Father's Will is expressed through the energy of love rays. You are the self-realized person who wants to help others become motivated through love as you are. You recognize the perfection of each soul, seeing the perfection in others.

The Mars influence is a green flame healing souls that are disturbed.

Love of the Son

The second energy flow in the Soul Triangle is the Love of the Son, or Christ. This can be understood as the Love of the Son—the way we receive and express this love as it come through us—and what we do with it. You find the single digit (or Master Number) by adding the **consonants** of your first name. Use this number to consult the following pages to find the interpretations for your first name **Soul Love Number category**, which is influenced by the Moon. This number will make you aware of your personality and how you distribute your love. This number shows you how you really feel about what you are doing with others.

Soul Love Number 1

You need to recognize love in yourself as well as seeing it in others. See yourself as a worthy, beautiful person filled with love that you want to express. It is okay to give love, but to balance ourselves we also need to receive it.

The Moon reflects your individuality. See yourself as a delicate silver thread connected with love to many people.

Soul Love Number 2

Your love is shown in the attention you give to people, plants, animals and inanimate things. You listen without judging; people trust you. Live this trust, do not deceive.

The Moon reflects your tranquility and gentleness with others in any situation.

Soul Love Number 3

The love aspect of your soul encompasses others with enthusiasm and light. You shower this golden ray on everyone, communicating your spiritual self to others without saying a word.

The Moon reflects your interest in people as you bring love and caring to many people. Your dreaming time establishes a line of communication with your higher self.

Soul Love Number 4

Love is demonstrated by the order, loyalty and quality you show. You can manifest love easily and show it to others if you do not pigeonhole your feelings. Let others experience your deep love of mankind.

The Moon reflects your devotion to your duty as you see it. Let this silvery light flow through you and out your fingertips as you touch to heal.

Soul Love Number 5

This number indicates a love of the good things in life, faith in your fellow man, and faith in yourself. You can stimulate others to venture forth and experience the sights and sounds on this good earth and knowing this helps you to help others.

The Moon reflects your zing for life and living. Do not hide your shining light as the Moon hides its dark side.

Soul Love Number 6

Your emotions and inner self are centered in love for your family. This love moves outward to encompass and heal others for they sense your inner peace. Let the healing ray come through but do not enter until asked.

The Moon reflects your harmonizing influence as this cool light calms the rushing wind of discontent.

Soul Love Number 7

Your love is projected spiritually in secret, for you hide your true caring self from others who need your widsom. Although you prefer to work alone, there are people who would share in quiet contemplation the secrets you hold. People can be betrayed, but what is that when there is so much to be shared in love?

The Moon reflects your wisdom and your reserve. Your dreams are the clues to your inner self. Some 7's are working on the inner planes during sleep and do not remember their dreams.

Soul Love Number 8

You see your primal energy as a way to reach your higher goals—not just for yourself but for others also. The opening or re-opening of your third eye increases your love for honest and trustworthy associates. You may suffer a loss of prestige if you are negative.

The Moon reflects your courage, determination and fairness.

Soul Love Number 9

Your love is expressed in devotion and your mission to bring others the human equation. You have a great concern for human welfare, the love of all mankind. Watch to see that all this giving and giving is not interfering with another's growth. We all need to "share," not "give" and "take."

The Moon reflects your unselfishness and brotherhood to all mankind.

Soul Love Number 11

You can bring your clairvoyant ability to usefulness by seeing other people's challenges. You can assist and guide others through your love and concern. Your inspirational messages can change lives. See that you live your inspirations, not just talk about them.

The Moon reflects sincere striving for the fulfillment of your dream of a perfect world.

Soul Love Number 22

You express your love in concrete structures that are filled with accuracy. These structures can be physical things or idealistic concepts. To you the universe is orderly, excellently planned, and co-ordinated. You want to have it continue in that manner. Be careful you do not insist that your way is best. Expand your visionary sense by at least viewing other's ideas. And remember all talk and no work make a big mouth.

The Moon reflects your ability to be essential to the preservation of our good earth, our metaphysical playground. Use your love in good faith, in diplomacy and always read the fine print before signing. Remember the money changers in the temple who were scourged by the whip of the righteous man.

Soul Love Number 33

Your soul's mission is to transcend the desire to control others through their emotions. Your dreams are about controlling yourself so that your mission can be fully explained to the people. Develop your auric sense, your inner sight, so love from the Son can come through you to heal emotions.

The Moon reflects the intensity of your emotional drive to perfect yourself.

Soul Love Number 44

Your love is expressed as you keep order wherever chaos abounds. Keep the incoming love stable; funnel it through your mastery of your mind and you will have the patience to explain the complexities of reforms in world affairs, or any other challenge that you seek. You cannot refuse your power, neither can you abuse it.

The Moon reflects mental healing qualities.

Soul Love Number 55

Your love is expressed by bringing sunshine into everyone's life. This is the number which expands the life force in others as well as yourself. You believe in the love factor and how it can bring enlightenment to all people. Do not gain mastery over anyone by using false light, and do not dim their visions.

The Moon reflects your generosity to all you meet.

Soul Love Number 66

Your inner self knows and experiences total love which you are eager for all to experience. As keeper of the flame of love, move into the marketplace to teach the important lessons of loving kindness to all. Share your knowledge with others. Do not hide your light under a bushel. The right words will be given you.

The Moon reflects the rainbow in your dreams—healing rays come through the prism of love.

Intelligence of the Comforter

The third energy in the Soul Triangle is Intelligence. The Intelligence Ray is the comforter who comes to guide us. It symbolizes how you use your experience and faith outflow. This is the combination of the Father's Will and the Love of Christ that you filter through your individuality and bring into sight for all to see. You find the single digit (or Master Number) by adding the value of all the **vowels and consonants** of your first name. Use this number to consult the following pages and find the interpretation for your first name **Intelligence Energy** which is influenced by the ascendant. This number will make you aware of how you can amplify your spiritual growth.

Intelligence Number 1

Your intelligence is displayed by seeing beyond material concepts. The glass does not glow darkly for you, it glows red for stimulation and activity in a garden of creativity.

Ascendant: You will exhibit creative tendencies toward all that you do, intensifying the energy symbolized by your ascendant. Do not let your arrogance alienate you from others.

Intelligence Number 2

Your intelligence is displayed through the rhythmic vibrations that flow through you. Harmonize the rhythms of sight and sound to love and you will be able to guide others through chaos.

Ascendant: You will enhance your diplomatic arts through love, intensifying the energy symbolized by your ascendant. International agreements for the end of strife can fulfill the promise of a thousand years of peace.

Intelligence Number 3

This is the triad of strength—the inventiveness of the 1, the patience of the 2, is combined with the communication ability of 3 and can move mountains of energy toward belief in yourself and others. Number 3 has the courage to rush in where angels fear to tread, because 3 carries the banner of the Lord in their spiritual work.

Ascendant: In any astrological sign you will express the beauty and strength of structure as long as you know where these vibrations are coming from.

Intelligence Number 4

Your loyalty shines through your intelligence. Your leadership takes the form of the disciple who leads by example, and people will follow you because they feel you can be depended upon. Your standards for truth are high and could be a little stringent when asked to evaluate for others.

Ascendant: In any astrological sign you will express the foundation for all truths as you see it.

Intelligence Number 5

You want greater excellence in whatever you do, so welcome others' opinions, see their goals quickly, and strive to coalesce all these ideas into a workable higher purpose. Change for the greater good is understandable; change to impress the ego is damaging.

Ascendant: In any astrological sign you will exhibit a venturesome spirit and will reveal what is given you from your higher self.

Intelligence Number 6

At the soul level you will temper evaluations with loving harmony. You have the ability to tell right from wrong, much as King Solomon was wise. Do not detract from the universal laws of mercy by forcing your judgments on others unless you are asked.

Ascendant: In any astrological sign you will exhibit harmony in all the relationships you choose to enhance.

Intelligence Number 7

Reach into areas where unknown truths are revealed. Intuition coupled with knowledge will help you create new philosophies through abstract reasoning. Use patience to spread your wisdom.

Ascendant: In any astrological sign you will exhibit a courageous search for truth. Your goal is to detect, examine, and then let your guides take you further into the realm of esoteric knowledge.

Intelligence Number 8

Your strength of purpose is harnessed to your intelligence. You have the power to express the primal force to gain your goals. This sounds violent but is only meant to help you understand that strength is needed to go forward to teach the universal laws. Use rose, the color of love, to achieve your ends and keep your ego in check.

Ascendant: In any astrological sign you can use this power for strength of purpose.

Intelligence Number 9

You have the gift of love and you spread it like a blanket to cover all the unloved people you meet. You listen to their stories, become aware of their misery and then hand them the love they have been needing for many lifetimes. Be careful about becoming merely sentimental for then you would dissipate your goodwill with aimlessness.

Ascendant: In any astrological sign you will show your love for your fellow men and women.

Intelligence Number 11

Your idealistic nature and magnetic personality will draw people to you. People feel you have answers for them for they sense your psychic ability to discern the future. You can reveal truths of mystic philosophy when you find the fine balance between fantasy and reality.

Ascendant: In any astrological sign you will reveal your intuition.

Intelligence Number 22

You design and structure hope and fulfillment through intelligence. You have the potential energy to perform great deeds and selfless accomplishments unless you turn away from metaphysical concepts and take the road leading to greed.

Ascendant: In any astrological sign you will exhibit physical mastery over your abilities, yourself, and your surroundings.

Intelligence Number 33

You have come here to demonstrate mastery over human emotions and pass this knowledge on to others so they can learn to live a freer kind of life. Use the deep sky-blue color for meditation to bring you the ray you need for emotional healing. The temptation is to use all this power to control people, and this could be the conflict between your ego and the master. There are plus and minus emotions. Some are good—like enthusiasm—and some are not so good—like being hostile towards another person. Number **33** needs to study the range of emotions in order to understand how to handle the differences—unless their numerology chart indicates they have balancing numbers.

Ascendant: In any astrological sign you will exhibit mastery over the emotions if you understand how to use them to uplift others.

Intelligence Number 44

Being on the intelligent ray of expression, **44** knows that the universe is uniquely planned and orderly. The universe operates in a rational and sane manner, nothing bumps into anything else when we think of our own solar system. In **44**'s zeal to prove this, they sometimes try to go further (they think) by using drugs to expand spiritual concepts. This could open dangerous channels—dangerous because the person may not be ready to handle certain vibrations at that time. Meditation and positive prayer are safer although a little slower, perhaps.

Ascendant: In any astrological sign you will exhibit mastery over the emotions if you are prepared.

Intelligence Number 55

This creative mind principle moves through the higher mind and brings the life ray of expression. This number contains the idealism of **11**, the dreamer and traveler in the higher realms who brings back to consciousness the understanding of a perfected life force; the mental mastery of **44** can put this understanding to practical use right here and now. The **22** inherent in this number is doubly blessed with the ability to build visible structures—such as writing the concepts he or she has been given—which reach the emotions of those he or she touches. The caution is to be careful and not to detract from others by invalidating their viewpoints. People are just where and what they are.

Ascendant: In any astrological sign you will exhibit life energy in abundance.

Intelligence Number 66

You are the instrument that brings love so others can see and experience this joyous experience. Let this expression shine through your physical eyes. Let it flow down to your fingertips so that in touching others they can feel the touch of love. This master number is a powerful source for rejuvenating the spiritual love part of our lives. You have the following energy to express: inspiration (**11**) plus life force (**55**) equals **66**; practicality (**22**) plus sanity (**44**) equals **66**; emotional mastery (**33** plus **33**) equals **66**; and **11** plus **22** plus **33** equal **66**, or **22** plus **22** plus **22** equal **66**. Study these interpretations so you will come to know your strengths and weaknesses.

Ascendant: In any astrological sign you will exhibit love energy.

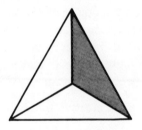

Mind Triangle

The Mind Triangle is represented by your second or middle name. You use the vibrations of the numbers that have been transposed from the letters. If you have more than one middle name, consider it one name. (This rule carried through for the first and last name also.)

The mind is a powerful instrument that you can learn to handle if you understand the different parts that comprise the whole. The Mind Triangle is divided into three energy flows as follows:

The Receptor—Superconscious

The Reactor—Subconscious

The Analyzer—Conscious

The Receptor (Superconscious)

The first energy—the Receptor—is the part of the mind that receives impressions. It sees and hears and records experiences you have. These experiences are stored very neatly and you can bring them to view at anytime you choose. This is done by remembering consciously, or it can be done by meditating or through hypnosis. The Receptor is likened to a vessel holding something—a receiver of knowledge from the physical world as well as from the spiritual world. You find the single digit (or Master Number) by adding the vowels of your second name. Use this number to consult the following pages for the interpretation of your **Receptor Mind** category, which is influenced by the planet Mars. This number will make you aware of how you motivate yourself to really see and experience life.

Receptor Mind Number 1

This is the creative mind that quickly and efficiently sees and experiences what is. Observations are catalogued and cross-filed for immediate use. A person with **1** as Receptor is usually specific, certain of facts, and can reach higher levels of understanding and awareness if he or she does not become arrogant.

Mars energy stimulates the creative mind.

Receptor Mind Number 2

This is a mind willing to take unlimited time to unravel the intricacies of philosophical discussions. It is receptive to others' ideas. This patient, sensitive mind can observe many things about people, becoming the intuitive who almost seems to read other people's minds. If this sensitivity turns sour and takes personal affront at unimportant things, **2** may become impatient.

Mars energy shows receptivity.

Receptor Mind Number 3

Communication comes easily to a **3** mind because it can pick up vibrations of others and can help others to become intuitive counselors. Observe and act are the keywords for this mind type. They express themselves with entertainment and humor. Overacting will dim the image of this type of mind.

Mars energy is brilliant in its observation of the inflow of facts.

Receptor Mind Number 4

Thorough and methodical **4** can manifest their needs with self-discipline and conscientious attention to detail. The rays coming from above enter the super-conscious mind to bring it healing vibrations for the etheric body. These people can be rigid which will limit their power.

Mars energy is expressed as a burning desire to place all things on a logical plane.

Receptor Mind Number 5

If **5**'s can discipline themselves they can develop their psychic powers. They are mentally curious and prefer to play the game rather than being the observer. They can use great reasoning powers to reach their goals.

Mars energy is active and involved, motivated by change.

Receptor Mind Number 6

These people have a stability of character which attracts others to their vicinity for evaluation of problems. They can see both sides of the problem, are unconventional and conscientious in their counseling. Emotions get in the way of **6** motivation and their cool judgment disintegrates when they interfere where they are not asked to help.

Mars energy is motivated by a desire to divide the sheep from the goats and remain impartial.

Receptor Mind Number 7

The examiners are ready to listen, as they want more information so they interrogate the person who is outflowing to them. When confused by overwhelming work or study these intelligent minds become skeptical. Their analytical ability can become annoying to others if it becomes too repetitive.

Mars energy motivates the use of wisdom, using a very fine focus.

Receptor Mind Number 8

There is a motivation toward excellence in the selection of employees and peers. This vibration handles money and prosperity very well. This optimistic power will help open the third eye. This number may also excel in sports. Physical and spiritual energy is not in conflict. Power, fame or glory can be abused if **8** gets greedy and ego inflated.

Mars energy energizes the determinism to succeed.

Receptor Mind Number 9

The universal brotherhood that is seen by the receptor mind assists them in interpreting idealistic viewpoints, love, and humanistic pursuits. This visionary concept of a better world is inspiring. Common sense and discretion can help **9**'s as they carry the banner of love.

Mars energy goes forth with love and zeal.

Receptor Mind Number 11

This "electrical" type of mind is capable of remarkable inventions. These people live on and yet are not part of the earth. As God's messengers, they receive inspirations from above and must share these revelations with others. They love their ideals more than they do the individual. Some **11**'s are asleep and need to rouse themselves to the exalted vibrations of the universe.

Mars energy sends flashes of inspirations.

Receptor Mind Number 22

In our computerized world **22**'s can become master analysts. Their ideas are solid and efficient and will stand for years. Responsibility comes with the territory. Negative actions can destroy the very things they want to accomplish.

Mars energy fires and ignites the energies of those they contact.

Receptor Mind Number 33

This part of the mind can switch from the abstract to the practical in a twinkling. Carefully prepared texts with a dramatic flair will catch their attention — they are receptive to the dramatization of any proposition. People are swayed by a good orator, so 33's need to watch their emotional control over others, for they may engender hidden karma.

Mars energy is governed by the flow of emotional exchange between people.

Receptor Mind Number 44

This Receptor mind is finely tuned to accept direction from higher sources. If 44's begin to doubt their ability to contact higher beings, it is truly "in their mind." For the sources are ready.

Mars energy is motivated by power and enlightenment coming from higher beings.

Receptor Mind Number 55

This clear channel receives from other dimensions the secrets of affluence in all things of both the spirit and material world. This Receptor side of the mind envisions life-giving energy that is pouring out to our solar system through the grace of God. This vision motivates 55 to greater efforts in bringing abundant life to all. Again, as with all master numbers, this amount of power and ability to move objects and people around can become a threat if used to obtain mastery by taking away others' life force.

Mars energy directs the fire of divine life force.

Receptor Mind Number 66

This Receptor is motivated by the highest resonance of the love chord. In this chord are notes of love which vibrate through the chakras to heal the hurts of neglect, sorrow, and fear. These hurts have been hidden from conscious view for a lifetime or many lifetimes. This love energy opens the channels to wipe away the distress with tears of joy. Do not repress your expression of love to others or you will miss out on the joyful replenishing of the living waters of love.

Mars energy directs the joy of loving.

The Reactor (Subconscious)

The second energy flow of the mind is the Reactor or the subconscious. The Reactor part of the mind reacts to stimuli, pain, injury, or emotional upsets that occur in either past experiences of this life or during past lives. This reaction can be pleasant or unpleasant. Those periods of time (perhaps only seconds) when you thought you were going to lose this body were moments of severe trauma. You acted in a certain way to preserve your life or the lives of others and this left a lasting program on your subconscious. This program or tape comes on automatically, just as if you had pushed a button on your tape recorder. You find the singled digit (or Master Number) by adding the consonants of your middle name (or names). The Reactor number is interpreted on the following pages and will help you see the hidden influences which keep you from experiencing the goals you wish to reach. This part of yourself is influenced by the Moon in your horoscope.

Reactor Mind Number 1

Your mind works quickly, reacts quickly, and you are willing to dare to do things. Some people will be disappointed in you for they see only the clown, not the seriously motivated person. When threatened, you react with calmness unless forced into a corner, then you come out scratching, rebelling against restrictions that (surprise??!!) may turn out to be barriers that you have erected.

The Moon reflects your courage and originality in handling traumas.

Reactor Mind Number 2

Here is the perfect person Friday; you know what your employer wants before he or she does. You keep the books, clear the decks, and produce ideas that are safe and sane. Your reaction to problems is to sort out the pros and cons until you have a detailed grasp of the situation, then you act and not before. Don't get so caught up in doing for others that you lose sight of your own identity.

The Moon reflects your sensitivity.

Reactor Mind Number 3

Here is a mind quick with repartee; receptive to new and interesting reactions—clean and quick and incisive as a rapier. Communication is the keyword as these people accept or reject ideas and pass ideas along with amusement and energy. Sometimes 3's exaggerate their predicament to gain attention.

The Moon reflects your interest in self and others.

Reactor Mind Number 4

Reactions of this mind are slow and deliberate, grinding slowly over all the ramifications of a problem. Or you become rigid in your opinions. You can pigeonhole each aspect of life, waiting to handle it at the proper time. Love can surface if you take time to look at the other person's viewpoint then let your emotions surface.

The Moon reflects your devotion to the concept of sincerity.

Reactor Mind Number 5

Handling several different occupations, languages, people, or problems is easy for you. Your reactions are quick to change. On the positive side, you can see several solutions to a single problem, your only dilemma being "which one shall I choose????" You inject life and emotion into your decisions, and can do creative healing on the mental level.

The Moon reflects your versatility.

Reactor Mind Number 6

This metaphysical mind is the doorway to higher mind through harmony. This means harmonizing yourself by studying, meditating in silence, or meditating with music and dance in order to bring your vibrations so high that your reactions to any problem will only bring peace. Be watchful of taking on another's karma by interfering where you are not invited.

The Moon reflects a harmonizing influence that calms the wind of discontent.

Reactor Mind Number 7

Here is an analytical mind that reacts to attacks with inner wisdom. This is the healer of spiritual gaps, the mystic who works alone and applies a scientific approach to problems and challenges. You take philosophical discussions apart and restructure opinions by using knowledge gained from higher dimensions. Watch your pride.

The Moon reflects your wisdom and reserve.

Reactor Mind Number 8

This explosive primal energy can react in a powerful constructive way, or in violent outbursts if things are not going as planned. Your all seeing inner eye can detect falseness and fair play. You can react to either in a dynamic way to correct or accept solutions. You can inspire others to do their best.

The Moon reflects brilliance and a positive approach.

Reactor Mind Number 9

This number carries a highly emotional reaction to the attitudes of others which results in a sympathic response. Your inner self wants personal love as well as impersonal compassion. You cannot be forced to react, you react through love, assisting all those who come to you for help. If this help is rejected you can become unforgiving and bitter.

The Moon reflects your loving brotherhood.

Reactor Mind Number 11

The intellectual idealist who hardly ever gets upset unless people try to push you into action which is against your principles. You prefer to dream about projected projects instead of putting them into action. Your inner self is constantly urging you forward to take care of mankind through some kind of instruction.

The Moon reflects a sincere striving for perfection in self and others.

Reactor Mind Number 22

This master planner in government and industry reacts calmly to criticism knowing that plans have been formulated already and are going ahead with vigor and diplomacy. Your intuitively intelligent mind knows your ability and power. Negative vibrations bring an inflated ego to the fore and big talk may reign instead of deeds.

The Moon reflects your mastery over the physical world.

Reactor Mind Number 33

Because of the emotional content of this number, you are apt to "blow up" in certain situations unless you have truly mastered and understood what has triggered you into reacting. A study of the emotional gradients will bring more ability to confront problems. You can transcend negative reactions and be the intense, controlled idealist with the power to inspire other.

The Moon reflects your intensity and emotional drive toward perfection.

Reactor Mind Number 44

This is the inquiring mind that begins questioning when triggered into reacting. You want to know how the other person arrived at such and such a conclusion. Your inner self truly wants to know answers and gets very frustrated if you are prohibited from consulting one who knows. You need order and constancy. Negatively, you could twist the truth in order to gain fame for yourself.

The Moon reflects the mental healing qualities.

Reactor Mind Number 55

At the highest level, you react to upsets with creative force to bring yourself into alignment with your true self. This can be done by breathing techniques, yoga exercise, etc. You instinctively know you need breath to control the life force when you are upset or you see others upset. You can also calm others by projecting your aura color of red-violet towards them. Do not take the energy of life or try to control others.

The Moon reflects your universal life-giving energies.

Reactor Mind Number 66

At the highest level, you react with love to the things that trigger your emotions. You do not project anger or hostility toward another or blame them when things go wrong. You need to remember that Master Numbers carry a higher energy level than the single digits. You selected your name before you were born, so you are vibrating at the correct number. If you have chosen this powerful love energy then you know that you can settle arguments with love instead of battle. You can see through anger and anxieties and assist others to come to a sane place of agreement.

The Moon reflects love energy.

The Analyzer (Conscious Mind)

The third energy flow of the mind is the Analyzer or conscious part of the mind. The analyzer is the part of the mind that is conscious—the part that thinks. This part is able to separate the whole into its component parts, i.e., is able to divide pleasant experiences from unpleasant unless a trauma included unconsciousness. The unconscious part of the mind is what we react to, for emotions are triggered without our being able to control them. The Analyzer is the part of the mind that thinks before acting. It is the observer; it is aware. You find the single digit (or Master Number) by adding the vowels and the consonants of your second name. Interpret the Analyzer Mind number to understand how your ascendant is influenced for this number will help you decide the direction of your desires.

Analyzer Mind Number 1

You are able to make decisions, see things clearly and will not let the opinions of others sway you. Work alone or in a position of authority, for you move ahead in a direct line toward your goal. You can analyze problems and challenges quickly. The new concepts that you are willing to try are sometimes a little tricky to handle and you might need a little assistance even though you are reluctant to ask for help. Let your ego go.

Ascendant: In any astrological sign you will exhibit additional creative tendencies in your profession.

Analyzer Mind Number 2

You can think on your feet like 1, but in a different way. You are constantly thinking of how you can effect a harmonious relationship with the people with whom you communicate. Your intuition and psychic ability can bring peaceful vibrations that lead to agreements between families, groups, and leaders. Curb your impatience and sensitivity consciously when making agreements.

Ascendant: In any astrological sign you will show additional tact in your profession.

Analyzer Mind Number 3

You are not afraid of hard work although you may impose on yourself in order to get your act together before you present your plans to others. Then, with confidence, you face the world, or your boss, and communicate the message with humor. You are able to work on several levels at once, which forces others to make giant leaps in conversation to keep up with your pace. Don't let your zeal leave too many behind.

Ascendant: In any astrological sign you will bring forth the beauty and desirability of the product or the project.

Analyzer Mind Number 4

You have a good grasp of mathematics. In the arts you would do well as a musician, for the technical handling of your instrument would take extreme skill. Manifest what you want by listing the things that are attractive to you—better job, new lover, mate, more money or whatever is important at this time. Also, less rigidity is required so that you can work with people and heal other's bodies with your hands. Do not negate this aspect of yourself. Study.

Ascendant: In any astrological sign you will bring additional organization to the outward expression of your healing qualities.

Analyzer Mind Number 5

Your analysis of any situation takes place with computerized transistorized rapidity. Your mind is like a sphere and you can move outward from any place on the circular surface with your ideas or viewpoint—able to change at a moment's notice. You can also move inward looking and searching, fearing nothing and ready for the challenge.

Ascendant: In any astrological sign you will face challenges with solutions and courage.

Analyzer Mind Number 6

You seek facts, not rumors, and then carefully analyze both sides of the question in order to exercise the wisdom and caring of King Solomon. As you exercise loving evaluation, life becomes the doorway to higher mind through harmonious relationships. Your fulfillment of your mission in this lifetime brings joy of self-realization if you do not interfere where you are not wanted.

Ascendant: In any astrological sign you will show loving impartiality.

Analyzer Mind Number 7

You work best alone and in silence (and you can create your own silence) so that your analytical mind can search and research the many fields that interest you. You can become the healer of spiritual gaps by applying your mystical knowledge to your mundane knowledge, and teaching what you know. Be truthful and use patience in your communicating.

Ascendant: In any astrological sign you will take the role of searcher and counselor.

Analyzer Mind Number 8

You are generous and dependable in your dealings with others. You know your own leadership qualities and how to direct your energies. Your energy can be directed toward success in business or success in the power available to you because of your study of metaphysics. Open or re-open your third eye and gain the knowledge of how to read auras. Use this power only for good or it will backfire.

Ascendant: In any astrological sign you will exhibit the necessary power to reach your goals.

Analyzer Mind Number 9

Your intuition and the broadness of your analytical processes will attract and inspire confidence. Your universal appeal can get results in areas where others fail since you are an interpreter of the greatness of life. This true humanitarian vibration understands the human condition and can analyze the way to use this knowledge to better the circumstances of others. Be aware of people who draw too much on these loving vibrations to your detriment.

Ascendant: In any astrological sign you will show love to your fellow men and women.

Analyzer Mind Number 11

You are able to do two tasks at once, cooperating on two levels as you communicate ideas in both a practical and idealistic manner. It is not necessary to analyze the situation as you know psychically what is going on. You may feel that you need to catalogue your ideas, laboriously writing lesson plans, etc.; then when you express your ideas, you flow with the inspirations you receive at the moment.

Ascendant: In any astrological sign you will express additional intuition.

Analyzer Mind Number 22

You will open new fields of endeavor and work out details to reach goals you propose. Your dynamic aura extends to include groups and you have the ability to analyze both the physical and mental side of any gathering in order to move the meeting toward realistic goals. Do not lose sight of your potential energy for great deeds and selfless accomplishments.

Ascendant: In any astrological sign you will exhibit additional strength of purpose and intelligence.

Analyzer Mind Number 33

You can analyze each emotion, dissect it and then understand how and why people react to certain other people. Our emotions are reactions to experiences. The causes of these experiences can be understood so we can erase programming. Study and learn to express the true mastery of emotions. Teach people how to do this also. Do not try to control others through this powerful number.

Ascendant: In any astrological sign you will express and teach mastery of the emotions.

Analyzer Mind Number 44

This reasonable, sane approach to life can be either analytical or intuitional. As a channel for higher knowledge from the mental realm, you express clarity of thought in speaking, writing or in some art form (perhaps as a hobby) that becomes delightful. People may expect you to be stodgy because of your serious mien, the way you hold your body, the way you act—then comes the explosion of humor. Stay away from mind-expanding (??) assistance (??).

Ascendant: In any astrological sign you will exhibit mental mastery over any situation.

Analyzer Mind Number 55

You can analyze situations and apply your life giving force by using various healing processes. You are capable of assisting other people to regain depleted life force by just being in the room with them. You emit a radiance that is indescribable when you are truly on your ray of sharing your energy.

Ascendant: In any astrological sign you send the life force energy in abundance. Do not take away another's life force.

Analyzer Mind Number 66

You have the master love energy number which you express in universal love for all mankind. Your stable base of love precludes analysis of any situation as you will project love to all as long as you stay on the positive side of this number. On the negative side you would want to "stop" all genuine expression of love that flows toward you.

Ascendant: In any astrological sign you will exhibit universal love energy toward others.

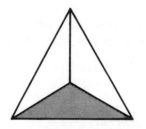

The Body Triangle

The Body Triangle is represented by your last name. You use the vibrations of the numbers that you have transposed from the letters. If you have more than one last name, consider all your last names as one. The body is the "house" we live in. It is run by the soul and yet able to function automatically as regards its systems. The mind can affect the body. In other words, you can consciously make yourself well or ill. The subconscious part of the mind (or reactor) can be triggered by sight, sound, smell, or any of the senses which will activate an experience you had in the past. If it was a pleasant experience your body rejoices; if it was an unpleasant experience your body may react by wanting to hide the truth—so it gets sick or crawls into bed pulling the covers over its head. When the three energy flows of the body (physical, mental and emotional) are balanced, the body is able to get well and stay well.

The body triangle is divided into three energy flows as follows:

Physical—the skeleton, muscles, organs, tissues

Emotional—the nervous system

Mental—the brain, our portable computer

Physical Body (Skeleton, Muscles, Organs, Tissues)

The physical part of the body provides the structure, i.e., the bones, muscles, organs, tissues, etc. You need something to help your body grow and stay alive so you give it food, water, vitamins, air, etc., to nourish it. You exercise and sleep to give it tone. You also may do some negative things—abuse it, bruise it, break it and overwhelm it with too much of something like food, drink, drugs, sun, etc. And all during this time of years you expect your body to stay perfect. If you neglect the body you sometimes have to have part of it taken away. Through this neglect, if you have too much taken away then you have no house to live in.

You find the single digit (or Master Number) by adding the vowels of the last name. Use this number to interpret your last name **Physical Body Number**, which is influenced by Mars. This number will help you become aware of how you treat your body and how it acts.

Physical Body Number 1

Sometimes 1's get too busy to pay attention to the physical body. You forget to eat or indulge in snacking instead of eating a balanced meal. You are also willing to experiment with new healing techniques, diets, exercises, etc., if something goes wrong. You can create your own rebirth. This certainly is better than tranquilizing your body with pills.

The Mars energy assists you to carry out the courage of your convictions about taking care of your physical structure.

Physical Body Number 2

This number is sensitive to incoming vibrations of color and music. Your body is graceful and rhythmic, flexible and bending to the various tones of the instruments. If you have this number and are a real clod, take a careful look at what you are doing to bring forth your talent.

The Mars energy moves slowly and rhythmically as it tunes itself to the vibrations of the universe.

Physical Body Number 3

You are interested in the body and adorn it with beautiful clothes, jewels and unusual colors. You are fastidious and therefore are usually faithful to the person you are with. Since you move quickly you may tire easily or confuse others with your sparkle.

The Mars energy is invigorating to most, which keeps the blood flowing and surging, relieving tensions garnered by **3**.

Physical Body Number 4

Hard work, either physical or mental, has no fears for **4**. You enjoy keeping busy and become the traditional workaholic unless your partner is able to bring the joy of playing to you. You are meticulous in your care of your body as well as the materials you use. Your toothbrush is always hung just so, socks are neatly rolled, etc. You take great care with food and vitamins, etc. You expect perfection in surroundings which can turn a lot of people off.

The Mars energy is steady, registering a constancy of intent.

Physical Body Number 5

Here is the traveler who loves to get the body in shape and take it to exotic places. You want to experience physical change, will exercise one month, diet the next, meditate the next, or seek another outlet to get into great physical condition. You also get a little careless and overindulge in many things like food, drink, drugs, and sex.

The Mars energy radiates to everyone who comes in contact with you.

Physical Body Number 6

This is a person who balances his diet, chooses the correct exercise and works on perfection with a routine that he follows exactly—unless he gets too concerned with other people and then he gets very involved with trying to help them. This is a great service, yet **6**'s need to remember themselves and their own well being.

The Mars energy is a fire of vitality.

Physical Body Number 7

If something goes wrong with **7**'s body, they can examine what went wrong in the past to get a clear picture of the cause of the distress. They don't worry about their bodies, or what they wear, or what they eat or drink. They accept what they are. They become restless if they are confined to the house too long because they like being outside in the sunshine and air. Esoterically this can also mean that they can astral travel.

The Mars energy cuts through the dross of opinion about appearances and gives you the confidence of being just who you really are.

Physical Body Number 8

You endure stress to the limit until it affects your nervous system and your wires get fouled up. You can—if you would invest 20 minutes a day—calm yourself. Or you could work out in a gym to bring yourself back to the reality of health. Your drive to create an effect on the world brings on this stress if the drive is abused.

The Mars energy is the material light that provides vitality for the body. Use this wisely.

Physical Body Number 9

You become so interested in the well-being of others that you forget to take care of yourself. You need to balance your energies and, remember, take care of yourself as well as your brother. The flow of love can become so intense that you need to let this energy out and you forget that you also need some stroking.

The Mars energy shines with the golden aura of perfection for self and others.

Physical Body Number 11

Since 11's are receiving higher vibrations they will need to take special care of the body. They are tuned to the vibrations of a select group of planets, which gives them an ability to share extensive knowledge with others. They need to get enough restful sleep and quiet meditation to keep their balance.

The Mars energy flashes, inspiring you to bursts of zealous endeavor.

Physical Body Number 22

This person exudes controlled energy, tightly reined. They are poised, composed, and know their strengths. Their carriage is erect and they walk with purpose. Their imperturbable manner sometimes keeps people from communicating with them. They have complete mastery over their bodies if they want to take command.

The Mars energy moves the cells in the direction of healing.

Physical Body Number 33

These people have very sensitive bodies. If you touch them when they are not aware of your nearness, they will jump as if jolted with electricity. Their subconscious stores old traumas very close to the surface of their conscious mind, so their reaction to shock is out of proportion to the occasion at times.

The Mars energy sees through traumas and is able to thrash out these problems.

Physical Body Number 44

This physical master has the power to heal with the fire—orange that emanates from the hands. You can use this power for yourself and others. You can also learn to heal the etheric body with magnetic passes over the physical body.

The Mars energy provides the fire of practical healing.

Physical Body Number 55

Since 55 reduces to 10 it has the capacity of attracting the higher mind for healing, you can use this power to provide life force for yourself and others. To provide this strong healing vibration you can connect the power circuits by laying on of hands.

The Mars energy is a lightning flash of healing power that brings in the universal life force.

Physical Body Number 66

This person can heal himself or herself with love—the power of universal love—not loving himself with ego. He or she can also use this energy to heal others.

The Mars energy is loving healing energy.

Emotional Body (Nervous System)

The second energy flow is emotional, represented by the nervous system of the body. The emotional part of the body is a subject for an entire book, but briefly our emotions trigger responses in the body which can be beneficial—like the emotion of love, happiness, pleasure, well being, and the like. These beneficial emotions produce a well-functioning nervous system. Emotions that are not beneficial, such as sorrow, anxiety, hate, or hostility, have a weird affect on the body. Some experts claim that being able to pinpoint the cause of an emotional upset will erase the emotional content of the upset and thereby cure or assist in curing a person's dis-ease. We have found validity in this assumption.

In order to determine your **Emotional Body Number**, you find the single digit (or Master Number) by adding the consonants in your last name. This number can be used to interpret your last name dormant-self category, which is influenced by the Moon. This number will help you become aware of how your emotions are governed and aroused.

Emotional Body Number 1

You see yourself well and strong, well able to withstand emotional shocks. Then you experience an unexpected trauma and go downhill fast until your creative self takes over and says, "I know what is happening and I will just have to program myself into wellness again." And you do just that!

The Moon reflects courage for if you picture yourself as capable and okay, this energy can be reflected emotionally.

Emotional Body Number 2

Your emotions are not easily aroused, but when they are your gentleness is laid aside and you reflect other people's moods. If a mood is negative, you "catch" the other's cold, flu, or whatever "contagion" is going around. Assist others, if you can, without becoming involved in their problems.

The Moon reflects your concern for others.

Emotional Body Number 3

You love good food, not particularly a lot of food, just expertly prepared and beautifully served. Your physical surroundings delight the eye. Your cheerful emotional outlook elevates other people. Be careful that your tendency to let trouble lie quiet does not cause others to acquire a frustrated sense of incomplete communication.

The Moon reflects your high emotional response to the positive energy of this number.

Emotional Body Number 4

You can manifest healing for your own body. With training in the healing arts, you could also learn to manipulate a body to bring it into correct alignment. There is a practical side to your intention and you usually control your negative emotions with just that—control.

The Moon reflects a practical approach to controlling emotional outbursts.

Emotional Body Number 5

You love to stimulate emotions with music or new sights, sounds, tastes, and feelings. You even accept the negative vibrations as being something different that you can experience for good in time, as you will be learning something new.

The Moon reflects your exuberant embracement of life.

Emotional Body Number 6

This calming, loving emotion keeps your body and surroundings in good condition. You heal with love as you face the real causes of dis-ease.

The Moon reflects a harmonizing influence on your own body and when you heal others.

Emotional Body Number 7

Your emotions run high for you have a real concern in the search for information about healing the emotional centers. You hide this very well, as your tendency is to be secretive about your powers of healing. Perhaps you are afraid of being sentimental?

The Moon reflects reserve and wisdom.

Emotional Body Number 8

You have powerful emotions that can be used in the realm of healing arts, or they can be misused to effect violence on others. You may feel that you know the right thing to do, and if your idea is compatible with increasing your vitality or that of other people, do it. If it decreases your vitality, don't.

The Moon reflects determination and powerful emanations coming from your third eye.

Emotional Body Number 9

Wouldn't it be great to look as young as you do and know that you can stay that way? Your love and emotions are expressed instead of being repressed. This activates a youthful appearance and maybe a few smile lines, but isn't that a nice face to show the world?

The Moon reflects your love for all mankind.

Emotional Body Number 11

You show a calm exterior which you have acquired through study and revelations. You see far beyond the average person, so potential emotional traumas hold no fear for you. You can handle them as a juggler handles his tools.

The Moon reflects a dream of perfection.

Emotional Body Number 22

You are the physical master over yourself, which means you can heal yourself just by talking to your body. Send your cells to the place that needs healing and instruct them to get busy and do the correct thing. An orderly life will help de-emphasize the emotional content in any upsets that come your way.

The Moon reflects an ability to control emotions.

Emotional Body Number 33

You have a tremendous emotional drive that depletes your physical resources. More attention is needed to diet, vitamins, exercise, etc., so you can gain control (unless you have already learned this lesson) of your emotions. This does not mean repressing them—it means understanding what causes the emotional flare ups.

The Moon reflects potential control of an intense emotional drive.

Emotional Body Number 44

You get upset if your power is threatened. Your emotions rise high and you lose your cool exterior. You have the power to heal mentally; don't waste it in trivia.

The Moon reflects mental healing qualities.

Emotional Body Number 55

On this level, the light from above infuses your body to heal any upset emotionally. You can focus this light on others for safe healing of emotional traumas.

The Moon reflects your spiritual healing.

Emotional Body Number 66

You shine forth a loving energy that can heal the emotional body. Love yourself as well as others so the healing rays can shine forth. You cannot give or share this emotional healing unless you yourself feel it.

The Moon reflects healing love energy.

The Mental Body (the Brain)

The third energy flow is Mental, represented by our wonderful portable computer, the brain. The mental part of the body is also a subject for a book! The brain is the instrument we use to store all the information we receive from the soul and the mind. This is cross-filed in unlimited categories, and the information on file is immediately available for our use when and where we need it.

You find the single digit (or Master Number) by adding the vowels and consonants of your last name. Use this number to find the interpretation for your last name **Mental Body Number**, which is influenced by the Ascendant. This number will help you to become more aware of how your brain uses its information.

Mental Body Number 1

Use your body to express your moods. Dance or any art form where you can use your original ideas would be one way to combine the mental and physical body. Your mental processes will activate swiftly without conscious thought to bring fluidity to your actions, whether they concern art or business forms.

Ascendant: In any astrological sign you will exhibit creative tendencies in your profession.

Mental Body Number 2

Your brain is a storehouse of facts and miscellaneous information that is extremely helpful if you have taken the role of the assistant. This applies to any type of business or role that you have decided to play. You have at your mind tip (instead of finger tip) bits of information that are very valuable. And you like to help.

Ascendant: You want to help others find the solution to whatever problem or challenge is presented and these qualities will be added to the natural qualities symbolized by your ascendant sign.

Mental Body Number 3

Although you seem cheerful to your friends, your serious side experiences anxiety. You plan ahead if only to make sure all your props are there. You use your facile brain to fill in any gaps that might hinder the performance of your plans. Intuitive counselors, such as you, are needed to help others.

Ascendant: In any astrological sign you will exhibit beauty of structure.

Mental Body Number 4

Your self-discipline and mental energy are reflected in your perseverance towards your goals. You express your ability best through material mediums. You could work with your hands, construct things or fix things . . . or people.

Ascendant: In any astrological sign you will exhibit some form of organized structure.

Mental Body Number 5

Your sexual responses are highly developed. Your fluid mental responses and processes move you from one action to another with swiftness. You see the advantages of change within the structure of many things and ideas.

Ascendant: In any astrological sign you will exhibit some form of change for progress.

Mental Body Number 6

Peaceful by nature, you will nevertheless fight for your principles. You are against injustice in any form. You are honest and reliable in your mental approach to problems. You have a therapeutic effect on people, because your objective point of view helps them see problems clearly.

Ascendant: You will exhibit harmony in relationships no matter what sign is on your ascendant.

Mental Body Number 7

Your lofty mental plane makes it hard for you to communicate with others. Metaphysical teachings will bring you closer to the source. You are the mental bridge across the abyss of chaos.

Ascendant: In any astrological sign you exhibit a courageous search for truth.

Mental Body Number 8

You have great physical stamina and coordination between your physical actions and your brain. This could be valuable in sports, your occupation, or in your hobbies which require the use of your body and your mental prowess. Develop justice and toleration for those weaker and less efficient than you. Lead by your mental strength.

Ascendant: In any astrological sign you will exhibit primal energy as you surge toward your goals.

Mental Body Number 9

Frequently you will find yourself expending energy in many directions, trying to help so many that you become physically and emotionally drained. Your mental side tells you that it can be done and your physical side says, "Help, I need rest!" Pay attention to your body.

Ascendant: Love for your fellow man will be added to the nature of the sign on your ascendant.

Mental Body Number 11

A balanced nature helps you adapt quickly to various situations. You can take in the situation at a glance, foresee the next move, and lead your contemporaries to a solution of the problem. You work well with others, showing both creativity and cooperation.

Ascendant: Intuition to solve challenges is added to the nature of the sign on your ascendant.

Mental Body Number 22

Constantly remind yourself that your practical mental prowess must be used for good. That does not mean supporting the weaknesses of others, it means not invalidating others' ideas until they are fully explored. Then the ideas can be refused if they are not compatible with the original plan.

Ascendant: In any astrological sign you will exhibit masterly intelligence for the solving of problems and challenges.

Mental Body Number 33

The mental attitude you have toward your experiences results in either a healthy or sick body. When you can control your mental processes and program them to act sanely, then you become the true **33**.

Ascendant: In any astrological sign you will exhibit your mastery over your emotions by your mental attitude.

Mental Body Number 44

You have the ability to heal through mental processes, delving into the mind, and sorting good experiences from the bad, and bringing others to sanity. Or at least to the understanding of their own responsibility toward themselves and others.

Ascendant: In any astrological sign you will exhibit your mastery over mental processes.

Mental Body Number 55

When you shed your light over the different mental processes that are available, you uncover some startling evidence about truth. Be courageous in your expose, knowing that your radiance will dim covert lies.

Ascendant: In any astrological sign you will exhibit universal life energy or life force in abundance.

Mental Body Number 66

You may feel that mental processes are not important, that everything can be done with love, and you are right. But what about the day-to-day living? There are practical things that must be done, such as balancing your checkbook. Use your tremendous love energy to learn about the mental abilities that you have.

Ascendant: In any astrological sign you will exude love energy to all.

• • •

As we discussed earlier, the body is run by the soul and the mind, the brain is only the computer. The brain, or the mental energy of the body, is an instrument for storing and cross-filing information we receive from the soul and the mind. The body reflects what has been stored in this wonderful computer.

In our DNA structure, our genes can be inherited from our parents, grand-parents, or great-grand parents, etc., and this inheritance will effect the body programming. Obviously every person with the family name of Rice, Smith, Jones, etc., does not look the same, or react emotionally in the same way, nor would they have the same abilities.

The interpretations of the numbers for the body provide clues to the programming of a particular "family" name. It is well to reflect on the separate categories of the soul and mind to see how these numbers affect the body number in these separate categories. For example:

Mary Ann Rice	Soul	Mind	Body	
Vowels	8	1	14/5	Desire
Consonants	13/4	10/1	12/3	Dormant Self
Total Numbers	21/3	11/2	26/8	Abilities

as compared with the following example:

John Paul Rice	Soul	Mind	Body	
Vowels	6	4	14/5	Desire
Consonants	14/5	10/1	12/3	Dormant Self
Total Numbers	20/2	14/5	26/8	Abilities

You can easily see that Mary's Soul and Mind numbers will effect the "family" name differently than John's numbers.

The preceding pages have provided a glimpse of advanced esoteric numerology and how it applies to desires, the inner self and natural abilities through your soul, mind and body vibrations. The mundane meanings of the vibrations of the numbers will also assist you to gain better communication with yourself and others. Stop, look and listen to the vital numerical vibrations of your name, for this is your potential!

Appendix

There are several services around that can provide you with the mathematical calculations for your natal chart. You need to provide the service the day, month and year you were born, as well as your birth place and time of birth. It is important to indicate whether you had an AM or PM birth. You only need to provide the name of the town and state or country where you were born (some people provide the name of the hospital!).

If you don't know when you were born, write to the Department of Vital Statistics in the capitol city of the state of your birth, and ask them for a "Long Form" copy of your birth certificate. If you don't ask for the Long Form, you will get a "Birth Verification," which will not indicate the time of your birth. The state charges for this service, so write and ask them what it will cost (usually about $3.50 or so).

The following companies and people provide astrological computing services:

Astro Computing Services
Box 16297
San Diego, CA 92116

Astro-Graphics Services
Box 28
Orleans, MA 02653

Astro Numeric Services
Box 1020
El Cerrito, CA 94530

Cosmic Connection
9250 Reseda Blvd.
Northridge, CA 91324

Rita S. Francomano
26 W. Susquehanna Avenue
Towson, MD 21204

Anne Hollingsworth
9398 Prospect Street
Honolulu, CA 96822

Minerva Bookstore
1027 Alma Street
Palo Alto, CA 94301

Bibliography

Avery, K., *Numbers of Life*, Freeway Press

Bailey, A., *Esoteric Healing*, London: Lucis Pub. Co.

_____, *From Intellect to Intuition*, London: Lucis Pub. Co.

_____, *Initiation: Human and Solar*, London: Lucis Pub. Co.

_____, *Letters on Occult Meditation*, London: Lucis Pub. Co.

_____, *Problems of Humanity*, London: Lucis Pub. Co.

_____, *Telepathy*, London: Lucis Pub. Co.

Campbell, F., *Your Days Are Numbered*, Bath, England: Gateway

Diegel, P., *Reincarnation and You*, Prism Pubs.

Fitzgerald, A., *Numbers for Lovers*, Manor Books

Johnson, V., & Wommack, T., *Secrets of Numbers*, York Beach, ME: Samuel Weiser, Inc.

Jordan, J., *Romance in Your Life*, Marina del Rey, CA: DeVorss & Co.

_____, *Your Right Action Number*, Marina del Rey, CA: De-Vorss & Co.

Leek, S., *Magic of Numbers*, Collier-MacMillen, Pubs.

Long, M.F., *Growing into Light*, Marina del Rey, CA: DeVorss & Co.

_____, *Huna Code in Religions*, Marina del Rey, CA: DeVorss & Co.

_____, *Secret Science Behind Miracles*, Marina del Rey, CA: DeVorss & Co.

_____, *Secret Science at Work*, Marina del Rey, CA: DeVorss & Co.

_____, *Self Suggestion*, Marina del Rey, CA: DeVorss & Co.

Lopez, V., *Numerology*, New American Library, Inc.

Rice, P. & V., *Timing*, F.A.C.E.,

——————, *Triadic Communication*, F.A.C.E.

——————, *Thru the Numbers*, York Beach, ME: Samuel Weiser, Inc. (a series for each zodiac sign)

Roquemore, K.K., *It's All in Your Numbers*, New York, NY: Harper & Row

Schure, E., *Pythagoras and the Delphic Mysteries*, Welby, R., & Health Research

Street, H., Taylor, A., *Numerology, Its Facts and Secrets*, North Hollywood, CA: Wilshire Book Co.

Thommen, G. S., *Is This Your Day?*, New York, NY: Crown Publishing Co.

Personal Chart Numbers for _____

Basic Numbers
Desire Number _____
Dormant-Self Number _____
Abilities Number _____
Karmic Number _____
Intensification Number _____
Subconscious Response Number _____

Soul Triangle
Will Number _____
Love Number _____
Intelligence Number _____

Mind Triangle
Receptor Mind Number _____
Reactor Mind Number _____
Analyzer Mind Number _____

Body Triangle
Physical Body Number _____
Emotional Body Number _____
Mental Body Number _____

Planes of Expression
Mental Vibration _____
Emotional Vibration _____
Inspired Vibration _____
Dual Vibration _____
Balanced Vibration _____
Physical Vibration _____
Intuitional Vibration _____

First Vowel _____
Cornerstone Letter _____
Key Number _____

Name _____

Birthdate _____

DESIRE

Vowels

Name

Consonants

DORMANT SELF

Total

ABILITIES

KARMA NUMBERS

INTENSIFICATION NUMBERS

PLANES OF EXPRESSION

Mental	Physical	Emotional	Intuitional
			Inspired
			Dual
			Balanced

FIRST VOWEL _____ CORNERSTONE _____ KEY NUMBER _____

INCLUSION TABLE

1			
2			
3			
4			
5			
6			
7			
8			
9			

Personal Chart Numbers for _____

Basic Numbers
Desire Number _____
Dormant-Self Number _____
Abilities Number _____
Karmic Number _____
Intensification Number _____
Subconscious Response Number _____

Soul Triangle
Will Number _____
Love Number _____
Intelligence Number _____

Mind Triangle
Receptor Mind Number _____
Reactor Mind Number _____
Analyzer Mind Number _____

Body Triangle
Physical Body Number _____
Emotional Body Number _____
Mental Body Number _____

Planes of Expression
Mental Vibration _____
Emotional Vibration _____
Inspired Vibration _____
Dual Vibration _____
Balanced Vibration _____
Physical Vibration _____
Intuitional Vibration _____

First Vowel _____
Cornerstone Letter _____
Key Number _____

Name —————————

Birthdate —————————

DESIRE

Vowels

Name

Consonants

DORMANT SELF

Total

ABILITIES

KARMA NUMBERS

INTENSIFICATION NUMBERS

PLANES OF EXPRESSION

Mental	Physical	Emotional	Intuitional	
				Inspired
				Dual
				Balanced

FIRST VOWEL ————— CORNERSTONE ————— KEY NUMBER —————

INCLUSION TABLE

1		
2		
3		
4		
5		
6		
7		
8		
9		

Personal Chart Numbers for _____

Basic Numbers
Desire Number _____
Dormant-Self Number _____
Abilities Number _____
Karmic Number _____
Intensification Number _____
Subconscious Response Number _____

Soul Triangle
Will Number _____
Love Number _____
Intelligence Number _____

Mind Triangle
Receptor Mind Number _____
Reactor Mind Number _____
Analyzer Mind Number _____

Body Triangle
Physical Body Number _____
Emotional Body Number _____
Mental Body Number _____

Planes of Expression
Mental Vibration _____
Emotional Vibration _____
Inspired Vibration _____
Dual Vibration _____
Balanced Vibration _____
Physical Vibration _____
Intuitional Vibration _____

First Vowel _____
Cornerstone Letter _____
Key Number _____

Name _____

Birthdate _____

DESIRE

Vowels															
Name															
Consonants															

DORMANT SELF

	Total		

ABILITIES

KARMA NUMBERS

INTENSIFICATION NUMBERS

PLANES OF EXPRESSION

Mental	Physical	Emotional	Intuitional	
				Inspired
				Dual
				Balanced

FIRST VOWEL _____ CORNERSTONE _____ KEY NUMBER _____

INCLUSION TABLE

1			
2			
3			
4			
5			
6			
7			
8			
9			

Personal Chart Numbers for _____

Basic Numbers
Desire Number _____
Dormant-Self Number _____
Abilities Number _____
Karmic Number _____
Intensification Number _____
Subconscious Response Number _____

Soul Triangle
Will Number _____
Love Number _____
Intelligence Number _____

Mind Triangle
Receptor Mind Number _____
Reactor Mind Number _____
Analyzer Mind Number _____

Body Triangle
Physical Body Number _____
Emotional Body Number _____
Mental Body Number _____

Planes of Expression
Mental Vibration _____
Emotional Vibration _____
Inspired Vibration _____
Dual Vibration _____
Balanced Vibration _____
Physical Vibration _____
Intuitional Vibration _____

First Vowel _____
Cornerstone Letter _____
Key Number _____

Name ———

Birthdate ———

DESIRE

Vowels
Name
Consonants

DORMANT SELF

Total

ABILITIES

KARMA NUMBERS

INTENSIFICATION NUMBERS

PLANES OF EXPRESSION

Mental	Physical	Emotional	Intuitional	
				Inspired
				Dual
				Balanced

FIRST VOWEL ——— CORNERSTONE ——— KEY NUMBER ———

INCLUSION TABLE

1			
2			
3			
4			
5			
6			
7			
8			
9			

Personal Chart Numbers for _____

Basic Numbers
Desire Number _____
Dormant-Self Number _____
Abilities Number _____
Karmic Number _____
Intensification Number _____
Subconscious Response Number _____

Soul Triangle
Will Number _____
Love Number _____
Intelligence Number _____

Mind Triangle
Receptor Mind Number _____
Reactor Mind Number _____
Analyzer Mind Number _____

Body Triangle
Physical Body Number _____
Emotional Body Number _____
Mental Body Number _____

Planes of Expression
Mental Vibration _____
Emotional Vibration _____
Inspired Vibration _____
Dual Vibration _____
Balanced Vibration _____
Physical Vibration _____
Intuitional Vibration _____

First Vowel _____
Cornerstone Letter _____
Key Number _____

Name _____   Birthdate _____

74/11/2		74/11/2		17/8	DESIRE 165/12	3	Vowels
55/1	5 9	5 5	9 55/1	5	9 3		Name
K A T H E R I N E	E L A I N E	L E G I N U S					Consonants
½ 2 8 9 9 5	5 5 3	3 7 5 1					

35/8	8	6/7	DORMANT SELF 59/23	5	Total
½ 55/1 2 8 5 9 9 5	5 3 5½ 9 5 5	5 3 5 7 9 5 3 1		8	

109/10/1   82/10/1   33/6   ABILITIES

INCLUSION TABLE

1	3
2	2
3	3
4	
5	8
6	
7	1
8	1
9	4

KARMA NUMBERS

4
6

INTENSIFICATION NUMBERS
55,11

5	3
9	

SUBCONCIOUS RESPONSE 7

PLANES OF EXPRESSION

	Mental	Physical	Emotional	Intuitional	
	AA	EEEEE	IIIR	K	Inspired 12
	HNNN		ST	U	Dual 7
	GLL				Balanced 3
	9	5	6	2	

FIRST VOWEL ___A___   CORNERSTONE ___K___   KEY NUMBER ___11/2___

Personal Chart Numbers for _____

Basic Numbers
Desire Number _____
Dormant-Self Number _____
Abilities Number _____
Karmic Number _____
Intensification Number _____
Subconscious Response Number _____

Soul Triangle
Will Number _____
Love Number _____
Intelligence Number _____

Mind Triangle
Receptor Mind Number _____
Reactor Mind Number _____
Analyzer Mind Number _____

Body Triangle
Physical Body Number _____
Emotional Body Number _____
Mental Body Number _____

Planes of Expression
Mental Vibration _____
Emotional Vibration _____
Inspired Vibration _____
Dual Vibration _____
Balanced Vibration _____
Physical Vibration _____
Intuitional Vibration _____

First Vowel _____
Cornerstone Letter _____
Key Number _____

Name _____   Birthdate _____

	Vowels
	Name
	Consonants

DESIRE 180/27 9

Name: R I C H A R D   R A Y M O N D   B A L L

Vowels: 9 (I) ... 9 ... 9 (55/1)
Consonants: 9 4 8 9 4 / 15/6 ... 9 4 4 5 4 / 26/8 ... 2 3 3 / ...

DORMANT SELF 130/3	8

	4	Total

ABILITIES 310, 58/13 4

INTENSIFICATION NUMBERS

KARMA NUMBERS

PLANES OF EXPRESSION

	Mental	Physical	Emotional	Intuitional	
					Inspired
					Dual
					Balanced

FIRST VOWEL _____   CORNERSTONE _____   KEY NUMBER _____

INCLUSION TABLE

1	
2	
3	
4	
5	
6	
7	
8	
9	

Personal Chart Numbers for _____

Basic Numbers
Desire Number _____
Dormant-Self Number _____
Abilities Number _____
Karmic Number _____
Intensification Number _____
Subconscious Response Number _____

Soul Triangle
Will Number _____
Love Number _____
Intelligence Number _____

Mind Triangle
Receptor Mind Number _____
Reactor Mind Number _____
Analyzer Mind Number _____

Body Triangle
Physical Body Number _____
Emotional Body Number _____
Mental Body Number _____

Planes of Expression
Mental Vibration _____
Emotional Vibration _____
Inspired Vibration _____
Dual Vibration _____
Balanced Vibration _____
Physical Vibration _____
Intuitional Vibration _____

First Vowel _____
Cornerstone Letter _____
Key Number _____

Name SHANNON LANE CLAYPOOL   Birthdate MARCH 1 1957

	61/7	60/6	67/12/4	DESIRE 188/17	8

					Vowels
	55/1	55/1	55/1		Name
S H A N N O N	L A N E	C L A Y P O O L			Consonants
1 8 5 5 6 6 5	3 1 5 5	3 3 1 7 7 6 6 3			

DORMANT SELF 118/10   1
24/6   8   86/14/5   Total

ABILITIES 306/27   9

INCLUSION TABLE

1		
2		
3		
4		
5		
6		
7		
8		
9		

KARMA NUMBERS

INTENSIFICATION NUMBERS

PLANES OF EXPRESSION

	Mental	Physical	Emotional	Intuitional
Inspired				
Dual				
Balanced				

FIRST VOWEL _____   CORNERSTONE _____   KEY NUMBER _____

Personal Chart Numbers for _____

Basic Numbers
Desire Number _____
Dormant-Self Number _____
Abilities Number _____
Karmic Number _____
Intensification Number _____
Subconscious Response Number _____

Soul Triangle
Will Number _____
Love Number _____
Intelligence Number _____

Mind Triangle
Receptor Mind Number _____
Reactor Mind Number _____
Analyzer Mind Number _____

Body Triangle
Physical Body Number _____
Emotional Body Number _____
Mental Body Number _____

Planes of Expression
Mental Vibration _____
Emotional Vibration _____
Inspired Vibration _____
Dual Vibration _____
Balanced Vibration _____
Physical Vibration _____
Intuitional Vibration _____

First Vowel _____
Cornerstone Letter _____
Key Number _____

Name _GARY BRIAN NICHOLSON_   Birthdate _AUG 10 1952_ _6:30 AM_   TORONTO

DESIRE 110/5 | 5

	55/1		55/10/1		21/3					Vowels
		55/1		9	55/1	9	6			Name
	G	A	R	Y	B	R	I	A	N	N I C H O L S O N	Consonants
	7	9	7		2	9	5		5 66/3 8	3 1 5	

DORMANT SELF 66/19/10 | 1

	23/5		16/7		66/25/17					Total
7	55/1 9 7	2 9	9 55/1 5	5 9	9 44/8 8 6	3 1 6	5			

ABILITIES

INCLUSION TABLE

1			
2			
3			
4			
5			
6			
7			
8			
9			

KARMA
NUMBERS

INTENSIFICATION
NUMBERS

PLANES OF EXPRESSION

	Mental	Physical	Emotional	Intuitional	
					Inspired
					Dual
					Balanced

FIRST VOWEL ____   CORNERSTONE ____   KEY NUMBER ____

Personal Chart Numbers for _____

Basic Numbers
Desire Number _____
Dormant-Self Number _____
Abilities Number _____
Karmic Number _____
Intensification Number _____
Subconscious Response Number _____

Soul Triangle
Will Number _____
Love Number _____
Intelligence Number _____

Mind Triangle
Receptor Mind Number _____
Reactor Mind Number _____
Analyzer Mind Number _____

Body Triangle
Physical Body Number _____
Emotional Body Number _____
Mental Body Number _____

Planes of Expression
Mental Vibration _____
Emotional Vibration _____
Inspired Vibration _____
Dual Vibration _____
Balanced Vibration _____
Physical Vibration _____
Intuitional Vibration _____

First Vowel _____
Cornerstone Letter _____
Key Number _____

Name _____

Birthdate __Mar. 1, 1957__   *Beechy Sask.*

I am?

DESIRE

S	H	A	N	N	O	N		L	A	N	E	C	L	A	X	P	O	O	L

Vowels
Name
Consonants

DORMANT SELF

Total

ABILITIES

KARMA
NUMBERS

INTENSIFICATION
NUMBERS

PLANES OF EXPRESSION

Mental	Physical	Emotional	Intuitional
			Inspired
			Dual
			Balanced

FIRST VOWEL _____ CORNERSTONE _____ KEY NUMBER _____

INCLUSION TABLE

1		
2		
3		
4		
5		
6		
7		
8		
9		